BOISE WITH KIDS

101 Adventures in Treasure Valley and Beyond!

By
Jean
McNeil

Published by Alturas Press
P.O. Box 1763
Boise ID 83701-1763

Copyright © 1995 by Jean McNeil
All rights reserved

No part of this book may be reproduced or transmitted in any form or by any means, electronic or mechanical, including photocopying, recording, or by any information storage and retrieval system, without the written permission of the Publisher, except where permitted by law.

ISBN: 0-9649-235-0-5

First Edition

Printed by
Catlin Printers
Boise, Idaho

Cover by Menzel-Higgins Communications
Boise, Idaho

For Kate

*My joyous companion, critic and consultant,
and my most excellent adventure.*

Contents

Foreword — 1

Using this Book — 2

The Adventures

Science and Nature

Introduction — 5
There's a good reason children are born scientists.

Touch, Please! — 6
Boise's hand-on science museum rates an A-plus.

It's a Trout's Life — 7
Under water at the MK Nature Center.

Make Way for Ducklings! — 8
Feed the ducks, beware the geese at Julia Davis Park.

Like a Hawk — 9
Pay rapt attention to Birds of Prey.

It's All Happening at the Zoo . . . — 10
Long-neglected Zoo Boise is getting a facelift.

Dig It! — 11
The Museum of Mining and Geology digs into Idaho's past.

Stalking the Wild Asparagus — 12
The sweet springtime vegetable grows free for the picking.

R-R-Ribbet! — 13
Take-home tadpoles to croak about in Boise's ponds.

Butterflies Are Free — 14
Metamorphosis before your eyes!

A Rose By Any Other Name . . . — 16
The Idaho Botanical Garden is paradise in bloom.

Cave In!   17
Journey to the center of the earth in Kuna Cave.

Down on the Farm   18
Boise's Public Market is the Saturday morning place-to-be.

Good Pickins'   19
Picking and eating is one of the classic delights of childhood.

Walk on the Wild Side   20
Where animals can be animals.

Star-Struck   21
What's up there and where to see it.

Autumn Leaves   22
It's not New England, but Boise's got plenty of fall color.

Say "Cheese"!   23
A bird's eye view of kid's favorite snack.

Smile! You're on "Sesame Street"   24
Behind the lens at Idaho Public TeleVision.

An Old-Fashioned Christmas   25
Cut your own tree and feel the spirit of the season.

Arts and Crafts

Introduction   28
Art for kids shouldn't be a spectator sport.

I'm Your Puppet . . .   29
Puppets singing La Traviata? Believe it!

BAM!   30
Serious art that's kid-friendly.

Music to Wiggle By   31
And serious music you don't have to dress up for!

A Moveable Feast   32
Now THIS is the way to peruse fine art!

Curtain Up! — 33
Family values take to the stage.

Tell Me a Story . . . — 34
When storytellers tell tales, magic comes to life.

Music Under the Stars — 36
Outdoor music with a light touch.

Paint Your Pot — 37
Masterpieces without the mess.

The Play's the Thing . . . — 38
. . . at Family night with the Idaho Shakespeare Festival.

Dance to the Music — 39
Ballet Idaho is more than a great "Nutcracker."

Encore! — 40
New public performances by a great traveling troupe.

History

Introduction — 42
History, Mom? First tell me what "tomorrow" means!

All Ab-o-o-ard! — 43
Visit Boise's past, present and future on the Tour Train.

Along the Dusty Trail — 44
Remnants of the Oregon Trail bring pioneers to vivid life.

It's History! — 45
This museum puts Idaho's past in perspective.

Bars and Stripes — 46
An inside view of the Old Pen can be fun -- or frightening.

It's the Law — 47
Where the governor governs and lawmakers make laws.

Assay This! — 49
Bars and two-foot walls remind us of our mining past.

Heart of the City — 50
A kid's adventure in Old Boise, complete with Pooh Sticks.

Train Lore — 51
The restored depot is a cool stop with a great view.

Basque in It — 52
A unique piece of Boise's heritage.

Sports and Recreation

Introduction — 54
A healthy mind in a healthy kid's body . . .

Down the Tube! — 55
The Natatorium is Boise's premiere swim spot for families.

Islands in the Sun — 57
Lazy summer days at Eagle Island.

Islands in the Sun II — 58
More lazy summer days . . .

It's Tubular! — 59
Floating the Boise is the quintessential summertime adventure.

It's Tubular! II — 61
This quiet float will have you feeling like Huck Finn.

Wheels — 62
Biking the Greenbelt on a quiet morning . . .

Climb Every Mountain — 64
Test your mettle on these mountain bike trails.

Take a Hike! — 65
Four kid-friendly walks on the wild side.

Get in Line . . . — 67
Roller skating? You mean roller blading!

Saddle Up! — 68
Get along little doggie! Ride the trail with these kid-friendly outfits.

Climb a Rock — 69
Mind your belayer and harness your energy on these walls.

Dribble, Dribble — 70
Bored teens? Send 'em out to play!

Take Me Out to the Ball Game . . . — 71
The Hawks play minor-league ball in a major-league setting.

Ski It! — 72
Day and night schussing away at Bogus. Nordic trails too.

Crack the Whip — 74
Childhood memories of figure 8's and scraped knees.

Joy Ride — 75
Coasting is a kid's thrill and a parent's headache.

Fairs and Festivals

Introduction — 77
Want something to do every weekend of the year? You got it!

First Night — 78
Ring in the New Year with art, music and your kids.

Pat that Drum, Hold that Horn! — 79
Symphonic music gets up close and personal.

Scrambled Eggs — 80
What's IN those eggs they're scrambling for?

The Sounds of Music — 81
Boise's Music Week has a long, harmonious history.

Orchids and Onions — 82
Hieroglyphics, silent movies and a pipe organ . . .

A Walk through the Past . . . — 83
Washboards are fun, but will they do the laundry at home?

It's Greek to Me — 84
Stuff yourself with food and music at the Greek community's yearly fest.

I'm Not Messy -- I'm Creative! — 85
What's not to like? Free arts n' crafts lessons in the park.

Pottery, Painting and the Past 86
Art and history mingle in Idaho's "different-est" town.

Get Soaked! 87
Eagle's small-town celebration just might leave you dripping.

So That's Where Milk Comes From 87
Fast-growing Meridian's Dairy Days harks back to the past.

Wild Rides and Cherry Pies 88
Emmett's Cherry Festival is the essence of a small-town fair.

Deli Days 89
The Jewish community's feed makes an unusual lunch break.

Take Me Out With the Crowd 90
If you like people, the Boise River Festival's for you.

Fiddlin' Around 92
They're rosinin' up the bow in the "Fiddling Capital of the World."

Fireworks on Parade 93
A pair of endangered traditions live on.

Ride 'em Cowboy! 94
Blue jeans and country dreams at the rodeo.

One More River to Cross 95
Hardy pioneers cross the Snake River in this annual history lesson.

It's Ba-a-a-ck 96
There's more than rides and games at this citi-fied country fair.

Art in the Park 98
Christmas shop with kids, dogs and artists.

A Fair with an Attitude 99
The Hyde Park Street Fair has always been a little different.

Nightmare on 9th Street 100
Forget jack-o-lanterns and bunny suits. Take 'em to the haunted house!

A Plethora of Trees 101
A winter wonderland comes indoors for a good cause.

Here Comes Santa Claus . . .   102
. . . and there he goes, riding in the Holiday Parade!

Deck the Halls!   102
Christmas lights? This year, leave the driving to a trolley.

Just for Fun

Introduction   104
Sometimes a kid just has to be a kid.

Play It Again, Sam   105
Work off the wintertime blahs at these indoor playgrounds.

Paddle Your Own Canoe   106
Too tippy? Pedal around the pond in Julia Davis Park.

Batter Up!   107
Some off-season practice for that Little Leaguer.

Go, Kart, Go!   107
They're noisy and bumpy, so of course the pre-teen set loves 'em!

Pizza and Prizes   108
Your money goes fast, but at least you can talk.

Preschool Play   109
This may be the best dollar deal in Boise.

Tee Time!   110
Hit a round or four on Boise's miniature golf courses.

Stayin' Alive   111
Downtown's alive with music, food and dancing.

'Round and 'Round They Go . . .   112
Kids and more kids at the roller rink.

All Wet!   113
Splash in the fountain on a hot summer's day.

The Silver Screen   114
Stay up late and relive your childhood at a drive-in movie.

Tag! — 115
Of course it's not a war game . . . I think!

Jingle Bells, Jingle Bells . . . — 116
Oh, what fun it is to ride in this two-horse open sleigh!

Day Trips

Introduction — 118
You don't have to go far to get away from it all.

More Good Pickins' — 119
Good scenery and great eating an hour away.

Huck Finn Time — 120
For a peaceful float, take your raft to Horseshoe Bend.

High Road to Heaven — 121
A rough road to a great pool.

Great Miners' Ghosts! — 123
Old Idaho comes to rough-and-tumble life in these "ghost" towns.

Taking the Plunge — 125
A mind-bending swim in bathtub-warm water.

Now THIS is a Sandbox! — 127
Hiking and camping in the spring? Just watch out for the wind!

Splash! — 128
Wrap yourself in a steamy cocoon after a day in the snow.

Soak Your Body — 129
Almost heaven at Idaho's signature hot springs.

Index — 131

Foreword

This book is a labor of love. Through my daughter's eyes, I have been privileged to return to the scene of my own childhood, and to catch precious glimpses of the childhood of today. Now, as Kate's journey toward independence accelerates, I am privileged to share with you some of the excellent adventures we have had, the lessons we have learned from them, and the lasting memories we have made together.

With Kate, I have returned to those long-ago places that had all but vanished from my memory: I've played games with half-remembered rhymes and rules, heard echoes from years past as a pebble hit the bottom of a well, stood with pride at the top of the monkey bars.

Most of all, I have seen how different her childhood is from mine, and how much they are the same. Today's children live in a very different world than we did, yet children themselves have not changed. My daughter still strives to understand herself and her world. Her play is still the play of discovery and delight, her adventures the adventures of joy, disappointment, success and failure. She is -- as I was, as you were, as her son or daughter may someday be -- simply, a child.

Kate is fortunate to be living in Treasure Valley, and I'm grateful to be raising her here -- where nature still teaches its timeless lessons, where activity is as natural as breathing, where friends and neighbors join in the rearing of our children. Here, more than elsewhere, we know the truth of that African proverb: "it takes a whole village to raise a child."

I'm grateful for the help and support of my friends and family: my mother, who raised me with love and courage; my husband, Don Reading, whose patience, understanding and computer skills appear to have no limits; the friends who shared our adventures, loved and cared for Kate, took my car pool shift so I could write, and listened to my woes. I also owe a particular debt of gratitude to three individuals who are also my friends: Jeanine Bohannan, whose fact-checking and critical eye saved me from many red faces, Kate Higgins, whose inspired cover art made me laugh, and Linda Watkins, whose generous last-minute proofing gave me the confidence to walk into the printer's shop, manuscript in hand. All remaining errors are, of course, mine alone.

Using this Book

Children, of course, wouldn't *need* to be told how to use this book; they'd simply open to a page and start doing whatever was there! But adults have both less spontaneity and more constraints, so we must plan. You can use the index to look for places or events you've heard about, or skim a chapter for the kinds of adventures that suit your mood.

The adventures are grouped in seven chapters: *Science and Nature*, *Arts and Crafts*, *History*, *Sports and Recreation*, *Fairs and Festivals*, *Just for Fun*, and *Day Trips*. Most fit nicely where they are, but a few stubbornly refused to be labeled. In those cases, I considered the adventure's primary purpose. Walks, for example, ended up in three places: hikes in *Sports and Recreation*, flora and fauna walks in *Science and Nature*, a stroll through Old Boise in *History*. Occasionally, the choice was arbitrary. Is roller skating a sport? Yes, I decided, if it's 'blading on the Greenbelt; a trip to the roller rink, though, is *Just for Fun*.

Where it was appropriate, adventures are organized within chapters in rough seasonal order; you'll find winter sports, for example, at the *end* of *Sports and Recreation*, Christmas tree-cutting at the end of *Science and Nature*. *Fairs and Festivals* is designed to be a resource you can turn to throughout the year: it's organized chronologically from New Year's to Christmas. Events are considered *Fairs and Festivals* if they occur once a year for two weeks or less; those that happen more often are listed in the appropriate chapter. The *Boise River Festival*, then, is a fair, while the *Idaho Shakespeare Festival*, which has a summer-long season, is listed under *Arts and Crafts*.

Day Trips are generally those that take an hour or more to reach; adventures closer to home are included in the appropriate chapter. Swimming at *Givens Hot Springs*, then, is a *Day Trip*; swimming at the *Natatorium* is described in *Sports and Recreation*. Occasionally, however, an adventure some distance away is listed together with a similar one nearby; in those cases both are included in the appropriate chapter. Horseback riding in Idaho City, for example, is listed together with horseback riding at Shafer Butte in *Sports and Recreation*.

Where there are age or height requirements I've listed them; otherwise I've generally left the question of age-appropriateness to your own judgement. Children, after all, are so different: my daughter was at home in the water long before most of her friends were, but at 8 she still isn't ready for laser tag, even though some of her friends love it.

Not every adventure will suit every child, or every parent. Children who are scared of the dark, for instance, are unlikely to enjoy *Kuna Cave*; parents who want no part of guns won't like laser tag. But children generally benefit from a wide variety of experience, and families will find something to enjoy in almost every adventure.

Throughout the book, safety was a high priority. At times you may think it was *too* high, that I give you too many cautions. (I'm firm in my belief that young children shouldn't float the river, for instance, and that life jackets and bicycle helmets are a must.) But my job was to lay out the risks as I saw them; you know your child better than anyone and you're the one who can best decide what cautions you can safely ignore.

Boise has an abundance of resources for families. Many are detailed in the book, but a few warrant special mention. For lessons, camps and clinics, the *Boise City Department of Parks and Recreation*, the *Boise Family YMCA*, *BSU's Outdoor Adventure Program* and *Community Education*. For educational toys, *The Children's Store*, *Discovery Cellar*, *Hobby Town*, *Ralph's Toys and Hobbies*, *Scientific Wizardry*, *Toycrafters World* and the shops at the *Discovery Center*, *Historical Museum*, *Art Museum*, *Zoo* and *World Center for Birds of Prey*. For school supplies and hard-to-find toys, *Creative Choice*, *Idaho Book and School Supply* and *Teacher's Pet*. For books, the 100-year-old *Book Shop* downtown is a classic; also try *Vista Book Gallery*, *Kid Stuff*, *Bookstar*, *Hastings*, *B. Dalton*, *Waldenbooks* and specialized stores.

The information in this book was accurate as of September 1995. Adventures like these change quickly and often, however, so it's always wise to call ahead before embarking. A second edition of this book is already in the planning stages, so please me send your comments, corrections, and -- especially -- ideas. Many happy adventures!

*Science and Nature*

Introduction

It's not by chance that we begin our adventures in the natural world. From the first moment of life, a baby struggles for control: of itself, of others, of the world around it. From the first time he finds his own fingers to her first mouthful of dirt, from tying shoes to learning to share, mastery of one's self and one's environment is the great task of childhood. It's no wonder, then, that children are born scientists: when they pour water, dig up a plant, taste dirt or care for a pet, they're learning how the world works and where they fit in it.

Children learn about nature in books and classrooms, of course. (Show me a preschool that *doesn't* grow beans!) But it's often the thing they get least of there, and in any case the natural world is best explored up close and personal. It's the perfect place for family adventure.

In this chapter you'll find new adventures in familiar places, familiar adventures in new places, and new adventures altogether. You'll laugh at lemurs, face a fish, nose a rose and check out the cheese; you'll go underground, up a tree and behind a camera; stalk asparagus, gaze at the heavens, raise tadpoles and cut your own Christmas tree. And none of these adventures will set you back much: in the natural world at least, curiosity is your most important passport.

If it's a success, this chapter will do more than entertain and educate: it will pique your curiosity enough to send you beyond the limits of this book. You may venture farther afield, to dig fossils in Clarkia, cruise the lunar landscape at Craters of the Moon, hunt for star garnets at Emerald Creek or count the waterfalls at Thousand Springs. Or you may prompt your child's class to venture places individual families can't go: on a tour of a bakery, perhaps, or behind the scenes at a newspaper or computer chip plant. In the natural world, the sky is indeed the limit.

❈ ❈ ❈

Touch, Please!

The Discovery Center of Idaho
131 W. Myrtle
343-9895

The **Discovery Center of Idaho** may well be, per capita, the best children's science museum in the country. It's an adventure you'll want to have again and again as exhibits change and your children grow.

This isn't a museum in the traditional sense: everything here is "hands-on." Kids see how air works by balancing a ball and blowing huge soap bubbles, explore the senses by testing their hearing or picking out familiar smells, learn principles of physics by building a freestanding arch, watch electricity in action by completing circuits.

The 150 exhibits are mostly first rate, and new ones are added often enough to keep everyone on their toes. The bubble wall is always popular, as are a pair of dishes that send whispers the length of the room; a "camera obscura" that brings the outside in, a room where shadows linger on the wall and an electricity exhibit where kids make bells ring and lights light. Our only gripe is that the phenomena often tax our limited knowledge; some simple explanations might be in order -- on lift-up plaques, perhaps, so as not to hinder discovery.

DCI hosts frequent special exhibits (animated dinosaurs were a big hit; the miniature planetarium is our favorite) and offers frequent classes and day camps for children ages 6 to 12. The excellent shop carries fascinating educational "toys" you won't see anywhere else.

DCI began as a project of the Junior League. The non-profit corporation opened its doors in 1988 with 31 exhibits, and has been growing ever since. It hosts about 90,000 visitors a year, and is open from 10 to 5 Tuesday through Saturday (9 to 5 on weekdays in the winter) and from noon to 5 on Sunday. Admission is $4 for adults and $2.50 for kids 3-18; babies and toddlers are free. Even better is the annual membership: at $35, it's a real bargain for inquisitive families.

❋ ❋ ❋

Science and Nature

It's a Trout's Life

**MK Nature Center
600 S. Walnut
368-6060 or 334-2225**

Ever wonder what lies beneath the Boise River? An afternoon at the **Morrison Knudsen Nature Center** will open your eyes.

The star attraction of the center's 4.5 acres is a 550-foot stream equipped with four viewing windows: at the two shelter windows, fish laze under logs, feeding on passing insects; at the riffle window, water splashing over rocks adds critical oxygen to the river; at the egg window, gravel shelters the little pink "peas" that will soon become "fry." ("Small fry"!) Signs at each window explain the process and identify the fish.

But there's a lot more here than trout. Pick up a brochure and a map at the Visitors Center and stroll the paved path: you'll see how farmers use their fields to feed and house game birds, how snags help birds and insects hunt and nest, how wetlands lined with cattails and willows shelter young fish, and how logjams help protect them. There's a replica of Idaho's high desert, an alpine lake where trout and salmon swim, the waterfall that feeds the stream, and a pond alive with ducks, geese, trout and even a huge sturgeon. At hummingbird and butterfly gardens, and at a model "backyard," you'll pick up dozens of ideas to make your own space more creature-friendly.

What's inside the *Visitors Center* doesn't quite live up to what's outside, but it's still worth seeing: warm and cold water aquaria, a bear den just made for crawling in ("Mom, it's so small!"), a "feely" box with feathers, snake skins and other remnants of nature. A model of the Boise River helps put things in perspective, and you'll leave with a better understanding of just how dependent we are on our precious water resources. But don't leave before you check the mural on the wall: those deer, owl and otter eyes seem to follow you!

Originally funded in 1990 as a Centennial project by the Morrison Knudsen Corporation and others in the community, the Nature Center is now run by the Idaho Department of Fish and Game. The walkway is open daily from sunrise to sunset; the Visitors Center is open from 10 to 5 and has restrooms. *The Visitors Center is closed on Monday.*

Admission to the Visitors Center is $1.25 for adults, $.75 for teens and $.50 for kids from 6 to 12. Toddlers and preschoolers get in free. The walk is free too, but please leave a donation if you can. And do check the excellent *children's nature programs*, including guided walks, Wildlife Wednesdays and a "Critter Club" for kids from 4 to 11.

❀ ❀ ❀

Make Way for Ducklings!

The Duck Pond
Julia Davis Park

Don your old clothes, pack a picnic lunch, leave your watch at home and head for **Julia Davis Park**. You can easily spend an entire relaxing day here, sampling the park's many attractions.

Start at the pond near the park's east end. Pack extra bread and you'll have no trouble attracting friends of the feathered persuasion. But note that there are geese here as well as ducks, and geese can be quite aggressive in the presence of food. My frightened 2-year-old and I spent one memorable picnic lunch eating in the car, so caveat emptor. (You can also feed the ducks and beware the geese at *Ann Morrison Park*.)

After you've lunched, head west to the *Fun Spot* for a boat ride (p. 106), a round of miniature golf (p. 110) or a ride on the carousel. On a more educational note, check out *Zoo Boise* (p. 10) the *Discovery Center* (p. 6), the *Idaho Historical Museum* (p. 45), the *Boise Art Museum* (p. 30), the *Boise Tour Train* (p. 43) or the *Boise Public Library* (p. 34). The park's *playground* was removed in 1995 for safety reasons, and was scheduled to be replaced as we went to press.

❀ ❀ ❀

Science and Nature

Like a Hawk

World Center for Birds of Prey
5666 W. Flying Hawk Lane
362-8687

The **World Center for Birds of Prey** is, first and foremost, a first-class research facility -- one that has been enormously successful in the breeding, care and study of raptors. The only Harpy Eagles to survive in captivity were hatched here, and the center was largely responsible for the Peregrine Falcon's removal from the Endangered Species list. Happily for the general public, and Boise's kids in particular, there is an excellent interpretive center attached to the facility.

Inside the center you'll see baby Peregrines and eggs in an incubator, hawks and falcons on staff members' arms and breeding pairs of Peregrines and Harpy Eagles. (Children may be less than delighted to see the remains of the small animals they dine on.) A tropical rain forest displays snakes, lizards and tree frogs, and a wonderful map of the Western Hemisphere tracks the migration of various species as a lighted "tree" changes color with the seasons. (Don't miss that one!) For patient children, there are 3 shows as well: a 30-minute movie about the Peregrine Fund and slide shows on raptors and rain forests.

This isn't a good place for most toddlers, who will find it hard to maintain the quiet required in some areas. Children from preschoolers on up are sure to be captivated, though, and most adults will learn a thing or two as well. Your spare change will go to good use in the gift shop, where you'll find bird-related items you won't see anywhere else.

The center is located at the end of South Cole Road, six miles south of I-84 at Exit 50. It's open Tuesday through Thursday, from 9 to 5 in the summer and 10 to 4 in the winter. Admission is $4 for adults and $2 for children 4 and up; toddlers get in free. An annual membership in the Peregrine Fund -- with unlimited visits to the center -- is $50. Allow two to four hours for this not-to-be-missed adventure.

To see these magnificent birds in their natural habitat, devote half a day to a hike in the *Birds of Prey Natural Area* (p. 65).

❀ ❀ ❀

It's All Happening at the Zoo...

Zoo Boise
Julia Davis Park
384-4260

Boise's zoo is in the midst of a renaissance. Opened in 1916 with a donated collection of exotic birds, it soon fell victim to neglect. In the 1960's the Idaho Zoological Society was formed to save it, and over the last two decades an energetic group of animal lovers has breathed new life into **Zoo Boise**. New land has been developed, old exhibits have been renovated and new ones added, construction of a new entrance, gift shop and education center is underway and the ho-hum children's zoo is scheduled for a complete overhaul. Plans call for $1 million a year in improvements for the next 20 years.

Zoo Boise houses about 250 animals of 100 different species on its ten acres. Longtime residents (some still living in traditional unrenovated cages) include monkeys, camels, tigers, bears, bison, zebras, leopards, foxes, wolves, beavers, badgers, tortoises and birds of prey. New exhibits house alligators, otters, cheetahs, lemurs and bighorn sheep. While otter-lovers may be disappointed by the animals' ability to hide, the lemurs are always worth watching, and the bighorns regularly delight visitors with games of chase over and around their "mountain." The moose and birds of prey are worth special mention as well: unable to live in the wild, these animals have some of the most generous-sized enclosures to be found at any zoo.

Zoo Boise is open daily from 10 to 5 all year and Thursdays until 9 in the summer. There are indoor bathrooms, a concession stand and a gift shop. Admission is $3 for adults and teens and $1.25 for kids 4 to 11. Toddlers get in free, and Thursdays are half-price for everyone. There's also a family membership for animal lovers: at $35 a year, it gets you into more than 100 zoos across the country.

The zoo's workshops and day camps for kids are generally excellent, and their special events (*Zoo Daze*, *Beastly Hot Nights*, *Boo at the Zoo*, *Claus for Paws*) are always fun. As for the wooden zebras you see around town, they helped raised money for improvements. A new fundraiser, "Zookie" cookies, benefits the renovation of the children's zoo. You get a free child's admission with every bag.

Science and Nature

You can mix a visit to Zoo Boise with a ride on the *Tour Train* (p. 43), a round of miniature golf or a boat ride at the *Fun Spot* (pp. 106, 110), or a visit to the *Discovery Center* (p. 6), the *Idaho State Historical Museum* (p. 45), the *Boise Art Museum* (p. 30) or the *Boise Public Library* (p. 34). The playground in *Julia Davis Park*, removed in 1995 for safety reasons, was scheduled for replacement as we went to press.

❋ ❋ ❋

Dig It!

Museum of Mining & Geology
2455 Old Penitentiary Road
368-9876

Idaho is a fascinating state geologically, with a colorful mining history to boot. The **Museum of Mining and Geology** will open your eyes to the past and present of Idaho's landscape.

Located on Old Penitentiary Road off Warm Springs Avenue next to the *Old Pen* (p. 46), the museum displays photographs and artifacts from early mining days and exhibits of the state's spectacular geologic features. An interactive exhibit helps kids make sense of it all: they push buttons to see how various minerals are used in everyday life.

The museum is open from noon to 5 on weekends beginning in April and ending in October each year. Admission is free, but donations are requested and fees may be imposed in the future. A small shop sells gem and mineral specimens and related books.

❋ ❋ ❋

Stalking the Wild Asparagus

Southwest Ada County
Spring

Whether you like asparagus or loathe it, this is a great springtime adventure. Even kids who wouldn't *dream* of eating it love to cut it. But go soon, before development erases the wild vegetable entirely.

Its foliage looks like a fern, but asparagus is really a member of the lily family. It's long been considered a delicacy, and grows wild throughout the Northwest. In truth, though, it isn't wild -- or at least not indigenous. Brought to this country for cultivation, it's what botanists call an "escape:" attracted to the bright red berries that appear in late summer, birds "liberate" the plant by distributing its seed.

Timing is everything: a week too early and all you'll see is the fern; a week too late and others will beat you to the punch. Prime time is usually about mid-May, with the first spears appearing as early as April. Go in early May: what you see will tell you when to come back.

Asparagus can be hard to spot, but you'll learn to recognize the distinctive "fern" even from a moving car. (Two adults *are* useful.) You're looking for light, sandy soil with ample moisture, so the banks of irrigation ditches are a good bet. Orchards are good too, but get permission and ask if it's been sprayed. (You *should* wash everything you pick, but do let kids munch at least one stalk right from the ground.)

Likely haunts change often depending on what farmers do with their ditch banks. In general, the rural roads of southern Ada and Canyon counties are good bets. Drive south along Five Mile or Cloverdale and southwest from there. For a longer adventure, go south on Highway 45 from Nampa: there are good pickings across from the cemetery in Melba and around Melba Road as you near the Snake River. (It's not for nothing that asparagus spots are almost as well-kept secrets as fishing holes and hot springs: the pickings here may now be slim!)

For a full day's adventure, combine this outing with a trek to *Kuna Cave* (p. 17) or a swim at *Givens Hot Springs* (p. 125).

❀ ❀ ❀

Science and Nature

R-R-Ribbet!

ParkCenter Pond
Veterans Park Pond
Spring

Just what you need -- another pet. But tadpoles are free, easy to keep, cheap to feed, fascinating to watch, and when they turn into frogs you let them go. Can any other pet make those claims?

Before you grab your net and head for the pond, find a two-gallon goldfish bowl or similar container, add tap water and a conditioner to remove chlorine and let it sit overnight. (You *can* use pond water, but how are you going to replace it? Go back to the pond every time?)

Finding tadpoles is like finding wild asparagus: timing is everything. The season is longer, though; you can usually find them anytime from April through June. Try **ParkCenter** or **Veterans Park Pond**; if those don't pan out, check *Hulls Gulch* or *Eagle Island*. And be patient: it's easy to miss the little guys 'til you know what you're looking for. Your most likely find will be tadpoles of the Northern Leopard Frog, though Spotted Frog tadpoles can be found in colder water and you'll occasionally see tadpoles of the Western Toad or Pacific Treefrog in still, shallow waters. If you just can't find any, order a kit from a local toy or school supply store, or from *Insect Lore* at (800) 548-3284.

At first your tadpoles will need nothing but food (try brine shrimp from the pet store), a clean bowl and a place to hide. They'll generally take two to four months to turn into frogs, growing fat and fatter until finally the hind legs begin to emerge. Now's the time to put protruding rocks or pieces of wood in the bowl. It'll still be a while before the front legs emerge for the final push to frog-dom, but when it does happen it happens fast: within days the fat, sluggish tadpole becomes a slim, agile frog, complete with all the markings of the adult.

If you don't let them go at this point you've got a tougher feeding problem. Frogs eat insects, preferably on the hoof. You can tried dried flies, but we didn't have much luck and ended up letting ours go sooner than we'd planned. Still, it was still an experience we won't forget!

❦ ❦ ❦

Butterflies Are Free

Your Own Backyard
Spring and Summer

Compared to the slow metamorphosis of a tadpole (p. 13), the **caterpillar's** transition to **butterfly** is quick and dramatic: its chrysalis forms overnight, the miraculous changes take place inside, and if you turn your back you may miss its emergence. Different as they are, however, the two are equally fascinating.

Finding caterpillars (*larvae*, really; the butterfly equivalent of the tadpole) is both easier and much harder than finding tadpoles: easier because caterpillars are more common, harder because of the endless variety. Unless you want to raise moths, you'll need a book to tell you where to look and what you're seeing. Common caterpillars in this area include the larvae of Swallowtails, Monarchs, Sulphurs, Whites, Fritillaries and Thistles. You may also find tiny green eggs, which you can raise through the caterpillar stage to butterflies.

You can keep your caterpillars in a fine mesh cage, an aquarium with a screen top or anything that will keep them in, give them air and let you see them. Fill it with leaves, sticks and whatever they eat (probably the greenery on which you found them), and keep it out of the sun. You can also buy a "butterfly garden" complete with larvae and food from a local toy or school supply store, or from *Insect Lore* at (800) 548-3284.

"Metamorphosis" is from the Greek meaning "change of form." In some varieties the entire process from egg to butterfly takes less than three weeks; others winter as larvae (caterpillars) or pupa (cocoons). Caterpillars generally don't make cocoons the way spiders spin webs (though they do spin threads to tether themselves); instead they shed their skin to reveal the chrysalis beneath, which hardens into a shell.

Before that happens, your caterpillars will grow fat and lazy; then they'll migrate to the top of the cage, a stick or one of the walls, depending on the habits of your particular species. Watch carefully as they spin "silk" to attach themselves firmly to whatever they've chosen, then shed their skins. Keep checking the pupa for the next couple of days as its hardens, because some take on beautiful colors: the Painted Lady's pupa, for example, turns an iridescent gold.

Science and Nature

The moment you've been waiting for is almost here: watch them carefully now because the whole process of emergence can be over in just a few minutes. (One of ours was kind enough to emerge during circle time at kindergarten -- honest! -- but most are less cooperative.)

The newly-emerged butterfly will hang quietly at first, resting and pumping blood to its wings. In an hour or so it will be ready to fly. (The red liquid you may see is "meconium" left over from wing formation, not blood.) Feed your butterflies daily, wetting a piece of cotton, a paper towel or a flower in one cup water with two teaspoons sugar. And please release them: they don't live long, and they deserve to fly free!

❦ ❦ ❦

A Rose By Any Other Name . . .

Idaho Botanical Garden
2355 Old Penitentiary Road
343-8649

Got a black thumb? Unidentified growing objects appearing in your yard? Kids *dis*appearing when it's time to weed? Raise your gardening IQ with a botanical adventure.

Even children who don't know a daisy from a tulip will find something to treasure at this "living museum." The fountain in the plaza invites both play and reflection, while the grassy lawns and meandering brick pathways lead you seamlessly through rose, iris and herb gardens, into meditation and butterfly-hummingbird gardens, to a garden planted by school children and a trail through Nature's garden.

Staffed by volunteers, the **Idaho Botanical Garden** is in bloom from late April through mid-October. Spring is our favorite time, but try visiting again in mid-summer: if you bring your camera you'll be able to see how things have changed. Try wondering aloud why the butterfly garden is planted as it is or how many different scents the iris have, and follow up with a trip to a nursery to let each child choose a special plant.

You'll find plenty of parking, but only portable toilets. No food is sold and picnics aren't permitted. Strollers are fine on the walkways, but there's a lot of grass and you'll encounter some steps along the way.

The Botanical Garden is open Tuesday through Thursday from 10 to 3 and Friday through Sunday from 10 to 8. Take Warm Springs Avenue to Old Penitentiary Road and turn right on a gravel road just before the Old Pen. Admission is $3 for adults, $2 for students 6-18.

Nearby, you'll find the *Old Territorial Penitentiary* (p. 46) and the *Museum of Mining and Geology* (p. 11). The *Natatorium* (p. 55) is just west and across Warm Springs Avenue behind Adams School.

❀ ❀ ❀

Science and Nature

Cave In!

Kuna Cave
Southwest of Kuna

This hole in the ground isn't for everyone. Partying teens and college students have pretty well trashed it; there are cans, broken glass and cigarette butts everywhere, and children of reading age are sure to learn new words from the graffiti on the walls. (Have an answer ready when your 4-year-old asks, "what's that say, Mommy?")

Still, if you can ignore the trash and the obscenities, **Kuna Cave** is a pretty impressive hole in the ground -- and besides, it's the only cave I know about. It's big enough and dark enough to thrill some kids and frighten others, so let the buyer beware.

Directions are critical here: from I-84 west, take Exit 44 and go south on Idaho 69 (Meridian Road) six miles to Kuna, where the road makes a right turn and 69 ends. Follow the sign left to Swan Falls (the visitors kiosk at the corner may or may not be open); after 4.5 miles, go right on Kuna Cave Road. Two miles down, a small wooden sign with an arrow directs you left down a dirt road. At the fork, take the curving dirt path in the middle. The last half-mile is rough but mercifully short; you'll see a littered "parking area" and a round rock wall ahead.

Don long pants and long-sleeved shirts, lock your car, grab your flashlights and head down the 30-foot metal ladder to the floor of the cave. (An adult should *precede* each small child.) The ladder and its protective cage were built by the Army Corp of Engineers in 1985. A right turn at the bottom brings you quickly to a dead end, but a left turn takes you several hundred yards underground -- farther than you'll probably want to go. Watch for low-hanging rocks as the tunnel narrows and opens out again into "rooms." Roam around as long as you can stand it, then head for the fresh air above.

Some kids will love the cave and others will hate it, but they'll all like it better combined with another adventure: swimming at *Givens Hot Springs* (p. 125) or picking wild asparagus (p. 12). Don't try *Silver City*, though (p. 123); that trip takes a full day in itself.

❀ ❀ ❀

Down on the Farm

8th Street Public Market
8th and Front
May - December

Shades of Seattle! On bright Saturday mornings at Boise's **8th Street Public Market**, yuppies stroll the canopied aisle, babes in backpacks and toddlers in hand, sampling fancy breads, goat cheeses and exotic mineral waters. But exchange a few words with any of the friendly stall-keepers and you'll know this is still Idaho.

The market is great fun on two levels: it's a fine place to people-watch, and the next best thing to picking your own (see pp. 19, 119). On a typical Saturday morning offerings might include fresh herbs, vine-ripened squash and tomatoes, dried flowers, potatoes in every shade of the rainbow, fresh lamb and a luscious assortment of berries. You can listen to music, sample homemade jams and dressings or just relax with a cool drink. Located south of the Connector at 8th, the market is open 10-3 Saturdays, May through December. Look for a special Halloween celebration and a July berry festival.

There are other markets at *Franklin and Curtis* (Saturdays 8:30-1, June-October; 888-9777), at *Edwards' Greenhouses* off Hill Road west of 36th (Thursdays 4:30-7, June-September; 342-7548) and at *8th and Main* (Wednesdays 10-1, June-September; 336-0267).

Farther afield, there's a market at *Kings* on State Street in Eagle (Tuesdays 4:30-6:30; 327-0220), two in *Nampa* (Saturday mornings at 3rd S. and 12th Ave. S.; Wednesdays 4-6:30 at Dusty's Emporium, 473 Caldwell Blvd.; 466-9337), one in *Kuna* (Premium Idaho Popcorn, 102 East 2nd, Thursdays 4-6:30; 362-3624) and one in *Emmett* (Saturday 8-12, N. Washington and Park St.; 365-6056).

These are all established markets but they do come and go, hours change and they close early if they sell out, so do call ahead.

❀ ❀ ❀

Science and Nature

Good Pickins'

Farmer Brown's	Smartt Farms	Gipson-Klein
8025 W. Chinden	3030 W. Victory	Gray's Lane
Meridian	Meridian	Nampa
286-9319	888-3189	466-2379

The Berry Ranch
7998 Hwy. 20-26
Nampa
466-3860

Scott's Produce
18458 11th Ave. N. Ext.
Nampa
466-9337

If your city child has missed the joy of fresh-picked fruit still warm from the sun, make your next adventure good pickings.

Crops most often available for "u-pick" are cherries, strawberries, raspberries, apples and pumpkins. Strawberries ripen in May, followed by cherries and raspberries in June, apples in August and pumpkins in September. Beans, corn, peaches, blackberries and watermelons are sometimes available too, and each has its own special ambiance.

Even small children can pick strawberries, which grow close to the ground. Cherries require a ladder, but the feeling is great and you can bombard your little brother when Mom isn't looking. Apples are the same except you can't use them for bombs and you won't eat as many; the thrill of pumpkins, of course, is choosing your own jack-o-lantern.

Some of the best pickings are a day trip away in Emmett or Sunny Slope (p. 119), but Meridian has **Smartt Farms** and **Farmer Brown's,** each with a range of crops, small stores, hayrides and petting barns. You'll find animals, hayrides and a store at **The Berry Ranch** in Nampa too, along with strawberries, raspberries and pumpkins complete with Halloween maze. Try **Scott's Produce** for raspberries starting in late June, and **Gipson-Klein Orchards** for Golden Delicious apples.

Pick up a guide at the *8th Street Public Market* (p. 18), the *Boise Consumers Coop* or *Zamzows* and check newspaper ads. Call ahead, pick a cool day, wear long pants and sleeves and don't forget containers!

❊ ❊ ❊

Walk on the Wild Side

Barber Park
ParkCenter
384-4240

What better complement to the zoo or nature center than a chance to see animals in their natural habitat? Idaho is home to 350 species of birds, 100 species of mammals, 20 different reptiles, 15 amphibians and at least 60 species of fish. Many can be seen right here in Boise if you know where to look.

Start by checking out books with the help of your local youth librarian (p. 34). Pick a pleasant morning or evening and head for **Barber Park**, eight miles east out Warm Springs Avenue. (From southeast Boise, take Federal way to Amity, turn left on Healey.) Take binoculars to view the birds: eagles, great blue heron, woodpeckers, northern flickers, kingfishers. Along the river, look for beaver, mink, muskrats and red fox, and see how many species of duck you can spot.

Walk a mile west along the river (toward town) to a path through a habitat area managed by Boise's Parks Department. The two-mile path leads you just east of **ParkCenter Pond**, and at most times of the year you'll see hundreds of geese, a heron or two and maybe an eagle. Homeowners in the area have spotted deer, foxes, skunk and 28 varieties of duck. Take your camera along for great memories!

This adventure is six miles round trip. If that's too much for your child, talk a sympathetic spouse or friend into dropping you at Barber Park and meeting you 90 minutes later at ParkCenter. There are restrooms at Barber, but you won't find any along the way.

❀ ❀ ❀

Science and Nature

Star-Struck

**Blacks Creek Road
Bogus Basin Road
July-August**

Looking up at the night sky can be a special thrill for children, especially since it means they get to stay up late! To really see the sky, though, you have to get away from the city.

Before you do, invest in a little homework. Stop at the *library* (p. 34) and pick up a children's book on astronomy. Find out when the portable planetarium will be at the *Discovery Center* (p. 6) and schedule your night outing soon after you've seen it.

You'll want to time this adventure for mid-August during the Perseid meteor shower, late July (South Delta Aquarids) or early August (North Delta Aquarids). With a little patience, you're sure to see at least a couple of "shooting stars" -- tiny meteorites that burn up as they enter the Earth's atmosphere. Unless you want to examine the moon's surface, you'll see the stars better on a moonless night. Be sure to take a telescope or a pair of binoculars.

Your goal is to get away from people, so the best bets are north and east. **Bogus Basin Road** has the advantage of being hilly, which helps hide city lights, and it's a beautiful place to be on a summer evening (a late picnic supper, perhaps?). But astronomy buffs say the best place is out the freeway toward Mountain Home. Take I-84 east to Exit 64 and head south on **Blacks Creek Road** to a likely spot.

After you've gazed, consider stopping at the *Discovery Center* or one of Boise's better toy stores for a set of stick-to-the-wall, glow-in-the dark stars. And the next time you're on the Greenbelt, pay attention to the Discovery Center's signs. Assume the Center is the sun; the signs mark the relative positions of all the planets.

❊ ❊ ❊

Autumn Leaves

Kathryn Albertson Park
Mores Mountain Nature Trail
October

It's not New England, but Boise has some pretty good fall color of its own. And therein lies a sunny October adventure.

Start by checking out a book on trees from one of the *libraries* (p. 34). Among other things, you'll discover that New England's colors come mainly from sugar maples (scarce in Boise) and that leaves don't *turn* red or yellow or orange -- those colors are there all along, covered up by green pigment during food production. As that process slows down in the fall, the green fades and hidden colors emerge.

Then head for **Kathryn Albertson Park** on Americana Boulevard. Leave the bikes and dogs at home -- this park is for walkers only. Its profusion of colors is created by the wide variety of trees planted here courtesy of the Albertson family and the city: aspen, oak, ash, locust, poplar and dogwood, among others.

Ready for a drive? Get in the car and head up Bogus Basin Road 16 miles to the ski area; drive through the parking lot and stay to the left, following signs to the Nordic trailhead. After you go through the open gate and past the ski hut, it's 3.6 miles to the right-hand turnoff for Shafer Butte Picnic Area and **Mores Mountain**. Drive 1.7 miles on the *narrow*, *winding* road to the picnic area, where you can eat lunch surrounded by yellow aspens and spectacular views: the Boise Valley to the south, the Sawtooth Mountains to the north.

After lunch, take one of the loop trails: the shortest (a mile) has plant-identification signs and good viewpoints; longer loops take you to the summit for even more spectacular views. The area is well-developed, with indoor chemical toilets, water in the summer, lots of picnic tables and an excellent wheelchair-accessible section.

On your way home, drive or bike the streets of Boise's North End, where the big old trees pour forth a profusion of color. Happy leaf-ing!

❀ ❀ ❀

Science and Nature

Say "*Cheese*"!

Swiss Village Cheese
4912 Garrity Blvd.
Nampa
467-4424

Talk about mixing business with pleasure! At **Swiss Village Cheese** you can advance your children's education and have a good lunch at the same time.

Cheese isn't made from scratch here (the milk comes in from local dairies), but you do get a bird's eye view of how milk turns into one of the kids' favorite snacks. You'll see it poured into long metal vats, heated, thickened with enzymes, separated into curds and whey, pressed, cut and wrapped.

These "show" vats make mostly cheese curds, for the enlightenment of the spectators. The real action goes on in the automated factory behind them, where some *two-million pounds* of milk are turned into 200,000 pounds of cheese every day, for shipment to distributors, grocery chains and independent labels.

A specially-designed viewing room on the second floor offers a panoramic view from six large windows. Antique dairy and cheese making apparatus is displayed in cases, and old photos line the walls. A self-activated video guides you through the history of cheese making and on a tour of the factory. "Rosabelle" the robotic cow talks about what you're seeing, and reminds you to wave to the cheese makers!

Before, after, or instead, you can watch the action while you dine in the small cafe. Sandwiches, cheese snacks, ice cream and kid's meals are served, and all kinds of foods and gifts are displayed for sale.

Take I-84 west to Exit 38, the first Nampa exit; the *Cheese Factory* is 1.5 miles north, a big yellow building with "Cheese" in *huge* letters! From Boise it'll take you 30 minutes to get there, but if you're adventuring in Canyon County already, it makes a great stop.

❃ ❃ ❃

Smile! You're on "Sesame Street"

Idaho Public TeleVision
1455 N. Orchard
373-7220

Being *on* camera may be no big thing to your media-savvy youngsters, but how about being *behind* one? At **Idaho Public TeleVision**, they can see the world from the other side of the lens. They'll also get a look at the Boise home of some of their favorite make-believe friends, and if you've never seen a television station before you'll find out what it takes to bring you your weekly dose of "Mystery."

IPTV lives up to the "public" in its name by welcoming visitors almost any time. All they ask is that you call ahead, though I strongly recommend you get together with friends so you don't all ask for separate tours. After all, these folks *do* have television to make.

By almost any standard, Idaho Public TeleVision is one of the most successful public broadcasting systems in the nation. You'll see their two studios, the control room where local programs are directed, the audio booth, the editing bay where programs are pieced together, the art department, the scene shop, the makeup room and master control, where the buttons are pushed and the switches thrown that bring *Sesame Street* and *Masterpiece Theater* into your living room.

Your children will get more out of their visit if you arrange to watch one of their favorite programs shortly before you go, and talk about cameras, sound effects and scene changes. To avoid disappointment, tell them in advance that *Big Bird* and *Barney* don't *live* here -- they just send their programs for us to enjoy.

School groups can also visit the other television stations in town: *KBCI* and *KTVB* in Boise, *KIVI* and *KTRV* in Nampa.

❊ ❊ ❊

Science and Nature

An Old-Fashioned Christmas

Boise National Forest	Boise	Cascade	Emmett
364-4100	364-4241	364-7400	364-7000
Mountain Home	Lowman	Idaho City	
364-4310	364-4250	364-4330	

We've never enjoyed a Christmas more than the first time we cut our own tree. Lopsided and far from perfect, it was the most beautiful tree we've ever had.

Starting just before Thanksgiving each year, the **Boise National Forest** sells permits to cut trees in specified areas within its six ranger districts. They'll give you a map along with your tags, which cost $10 apiece and must be placed on each tree you cut. They'll also give you the rules: cut trees with bigger cousins nearby, cut close to the ground, don't "top" large trees, don't cut near the road, don't leave greenery, etc.

You can get tags at the *Boise National Forest headquarters* at 1750 Front Street, the *Boise Ranger District* office on Warm Springs just past Eckert Road, and Ranger Stations in *Idaho City, Lowman, Cascade, Emmett* and *Mountain Home*. Stations are generally open seven days a week from 7:30 to 4 but call first, especially if you plan on getting your tags out of town. There's a limit of one tag per person, and all tags are good throughout the Boise National Forest. For something a bit less adventurous, ask about cutting your tree at a tree farm.

So bundle up the kiddies, shoulder your saw and . . . wait! What *kind* of tree do you want? Your basic Christmas trees are either pine or fir, and here traditions part company. If you said "pine," you come from the "soft" tradition: the woods are teeming with them; you can practically take your pick without leaving the car. But if your family indoctrinated you -- as mine did -- in the proper "fir" tradition, you're from the "tough" school, and you may be in the woods a lo-o-o-ng time. (If you said "who cares?," your family obviously didn't imbue you with *any* tradition. If *you* said "pine" and *your spouse* said "fir," I want no part of it.)

Actually, both fir and pine are available in the Boise National Forest; it's just that pine are more plentiful, and you have to go higher and look harder to find some species of fir. In the lower and drier elevations (*Emmett* and *Mountain Home* primarily) you'll find Douglas Fir and plenty of Ponderosa Pine. If you go higher -- to *Cascade* or *Lowman* perhaps -- and check north-facing slopes, your choice should also include White, Grand and Sub-Alpine Fir.

Unless you're shopping for the mall's tree, you won't need anything more than an everyday saw; what you *will* need are warm clothes, snow tires or chains, a shovel, a tape measure and a good plan for attaching the tree to your car. (Here it helps to remember a lesson I learned the hard way: *trees look a lot bigger in your living room than they did in the forest*). If you don't have a pickup or van, experts suggest placing the tree on top of your car *with the stump facing forward*: that way the wind won't damage its branches.

Don't neglect your tree when you get home. As soon as possible you want to re-cut the stump and put it in water, so pitch won't seal the tree and make it unable to drink. Keep it in a cool place (outdoors is best) 'til you're ready to put it up, and give it plenty of water.

If you take this adventure with small children, you'd be wise to leave your Christmas perfectionism at home. Kids love to search for the perfect tree -- for about ten minutes; then they're ready to get on with it. So it may not be the tree of your dreams. It's the tree of your kid's dreams, and that makes it your dream tree too, doesn't it?

❃ ❃ ❃

Arts and Crafts

Introduction

Very young children have short attention spans and are too "immature" to be self-conscious about their own work, so art for them is mostly participatory: they can't sit through a concert or a play, but think nothing of drawing a "horse" that looks more like a pig, or slapping colors on paper and calling it a sunset. Sadly, that balance shifts as they grow: they become more able to absorb professional art but less willing to create their own, and art too often becomes a spectator sport.

Once they get past kindergarten they may not get much art in the classroom, since it's offered only by volunteer Art Parents. Exposure to professional art is likewise limited and unpredictable. A parent's job, therefore, is twofold: to expose children to all kinds of art in graduated doses, and to nurture and encourage their own creative outpourings.

Over the past decade, what was pretty much a cultural wasteland has given way to something approaching big-city amenities. It isn't hard now to find professional art for children in the Treasure Valley: museums, orchestras, theater companies, dance groups, even the opera, all play to young audiences. The trick is to find venues that suit their age and interests and won't break your pocketbook. In this chapter you'll find opportunities you probably never knew existed: to hear great music in the casual atmosphere of a rehearsal; listen to *Sesame Street* songs under the stars; see *Shakespeare* or *Little Lulu* without worrying about your wiggling preschooler; take a gallery stroll by old-time trolley; even hear scenes from great opera sung by puppets!

You'll find opportunities, too, to nourish your child's own creativity: by painting a piece of pottery, experimenting with batik or creating a Mardi Gras mask. And you'll probably find, as I have, that it's often these do-it-yourself adventures that leave the strongest memories.

Tickets for many performances are available at Select-A-Seat for a small charge. Outlets are located at the Student Union Building, the Pavilion and the Morrison Center on the BSU campus, in Waremart at Fairview and Milwaukee and at most Albertson's stores. Telephone orders can be placed at 385-1766 or 385-1110; call 385-3535 for a list of upcoming events. For a list of arts events that may or may not be sold through Select-A-Seat, call ARTSLINE at 376-2787.

Arts and Crafts

I'm Your Puppet . . .

**Boise Opera
516 S. 9th
345-3531**

Boise Opera fan Joanne Hoyt has a hobby: she makes and costumes puppets. Not your run-of-the-mill sock puppets these; they're fully formed, spectacularly costumed characters from classic opera: fantastic creatures like Madame Butterfly, Orpheus and the Firebird.

The good news is that Mrs. Hoyt will take her talented creations almost anywhere, if it will benefit the opera -- to schools, libraries, even parties -- where they perform scenes from their respective operas chosen for their appeal to children. The bad news is there's no set schedule; you'll have to call the Opera to find out what's on tap.

Sometime in your children's school career they'll probably be invited to *Operatunity,* a one-hour opera performance specially narrated for elementary and junior high students. Held in conjunction with evening performances, the shorter versions are performed free (a $1 donation is asked) for an invited audience of school children. You can let your child's teacher know you're interested, or call the Opera direct.

Boise Opera also sends its *Children's Chorus* into the schools on a regular basis. Auditions are held each September, open to kids from 4th through 8th grade with unchanged voices.

Tickets to regular performances are sold through *Select-A-Seat* (p. 28). At $15 to $38 they're too pricey for many families; if there's something your child would like, call and ask about student discount tickets: they're usually available, though they won't save you a lot.

BAM!

Boise Art Museum
670 Julia Davis Drive
345-8330

This well-designed museum is a good place to introduce children to the wonders of art -- in small doses, thank you, with a maximum of freedom and a minimum of lecturing.

Located at the west end of Julia Davis Park, the **Boise Art Museum** is permanent home to the Glenn C. Janss Collection of American Realism, and puts on at least 15 exhibitions each year. The first stage of a major expansion is expected to get underway in the summer of 1996, and will greatly expand BAM's offerings for children.

Your best bet is to watch the newspaper and choose an exhibit that sounds appealing. (We found one with huge moving sculptures; our 4-year-old was transfixed.) Go at off hours so your kids aren't lost in a sea of grownups, then let them wander and take note of what attracts them: it's surprising how early children demonstrate preferences in art.

If there's interest there, consider enrolling your child in one of the museum's excellent classes, and visit some of its events. *Art in the Park* (p. 98) is a good choice, but skip the *Beaux Arts Christmas Sale* if you have small children: it's crowded and intimidating, and there's a real risk of costly breakage. I don't recommend *Museum after Hours* either; it's very much an adult affair. Try checking out some children's art books at the *Boise Public Library* across the street (p. 34) and taking the *First Thursday Gallery Stroll* (p. 34) downtown.

The Boise Art Museum is open Tuesday through Friday from 10 to 5 and weekends from noon to 5. Admission is $3 for adults, $2 for college students and $1 for children 6 and up; toddlers and preschoolers get in free. Admission is free for everyone on the first Thursday of each month; watch the newspaper for occasional "kids free" days, and see p. 8 for other things to do in and around *Julia Davis Park*.

Arts and Crafts

Music to Wiggle By

Boise Philharmonic
516 S. 9th St.
344-7849

You want your children to hear good music, but traditional concerts are too long and formal for them. Instead of waiting until they're teens, try the **Boise Philharmonic's** open dress rehearsals.

The Philharmonic offers seven Saturday night concerts a year, from September to May, each preceded by a 10 a.m. public rehearsal. Unlike the evening concerts, where proper dress and serious attention are de rigeur, rehearsals have a casual atmosphere: wear what you like, stay as long as you like, wiggle and squirm as much as you need to.

The musicians clearly understand that they have an unusual audience at these rehearsals, and often interact with its young members. Since these *are* rehearsals there may be pauses or repetition, but that's really a bonus too: not only do kids hear good music, they get a first-hand look at the work and dedication involved in performing.

Dress rehearsals are held in the *Morrison Center*, in the same venue as the evening concerts. They haven't yet become impossibly popular as so many things in Boise have in recent years, though it may be just a matter of time. For now, anyway, you can still get tickets at the door the morning of the rehearsal; they'll set you back a mere $2 for each child, $5 for adults. Groups of 20 or more get in for half-price.

Tickets for evening performances are available through *Select-A-Seat* (see p. 28). The Philharmonic also offers an annual *Family Concert* (p. 79), music appreciation classes, instrument instruction and guest-artist brown bag lunches the Friday before each concert.

✎ ♪ ✎

A Moveable Feast

First Thursday
336-2631

In times BT (before the trolley, that is), my friend's daughter had no use for art galleries; now, because they come on wheels, she loves them. And almost by osmosis, our kids are developing a "feel" for art.

All year 'round, from 5 to 9 on the first Thursday of each month, some 60 downtown and near-downtown art galleries, restaurants and other shops sponsor the **First Thursday Gallery Stroll**, with a free trolley shuttling visitors from place to place. Many offer hors d'oeuvres, entertainment or both, and the atmosphere is festive.

Participating galleries include the *Boise Art Museum* (p. 30), *The Art Source*, *Brown's*, *Davies Reid*, *Dream Walker*, *Gallery 601* and *Galos Fine Arts*. Most times, a couple of galleries will have artists you can visit with, and perhaps a weaver, sculptor or painter demonstrating technique. Other regular participants are *Toycrafters* (which usually has a clown making balloon animals), *Kandor* (great appetizers!) and *From the Earth*.

The trolley begins and ends its run every half-hour from 5 to 9 at First Security Bank's *Spring Plaza*, on 11th between Idaho and Main, making stops all along its route to the Boise Art Museum. (While you wait, be sure to check the fish sculptures and other art on the walls of this cozy pocket park!) As long as your kids are controlled enough not to break anything, this is a great way to spend a family evening.

Arts and Crafts

Curtain Up!

IJA Productions
1020 W. Main
343-6567
376-ARTS (ARTSLINE)

Taking kids to the theater can be an amazing adventure, but it can also be tricky. How do you know the material is really suitable? How good will the performance be? Will the kids embarrass you by wiggling and talking? Because it's geared specifically for kids, **IJA's Family Event Series** takes most of the guesswork out of play-going.

These aren't local productions; IJA is a non-profit arts presenter, which means it brings touring companies from across the country to perform at the *Morrison Center*. Its season runs from September through June and includes a music series, a dance series and a roster of musical comedies as well as the Family Events.

Some of the tickets are pretty pricey, but IJA keeps the Family Events within reason: $10 a ticket, $30 for the 3-show series. You don't save money buying the series, but you probably get better seats. Tickets are available from IJA or at *Select-A-Seat* (see p. 28).

For adults and older children, IJA sponsors *Literary Arts in the Park* during the summer, where published Idaho writers read from and talk about their work. There's also a *Young Writers Competition* through the schools, a series of architectural walks in the fall, the *ARTSLINE* telephone recording of upcoming cultural events and the *First Night* New Year's Eve celebration in downtown Boise (see p. 78).

Several local theater companies often do productions suitable for children. Try *Stage Coach*, at 2000 Kootenai (342-2000), *Knock 'em Dead*, at 333 S. 9th (385-0021), *Boise Little Theater*, at 100 E. Fort (342-5104), or *BSU Theater Arts Department* (385-3980).

Tell Me a Story . . .

Boise Public Library	Eagle Library	Ada Community Library
715 S. Capitol Blvd.	67 E. State	10664 W. Victory Rd.
384-4200	939-6814	362-0181
Garden City Library	Meridian Library	Kuna Library
201 E. 50th	18 E. Idaho Ave.	1360 W. Boise
377-2180	888-4451	922-1002

The library is a magical place for kids, peopled with talking animals, wizards, and children much like themselves. When adults weave stories for them, the magic comes alive.

All six Ada County libraries offer free storytelling programs, year-round or during the school year. Most last about a half-hour and are geared to toddlers and preschoolers, but babies and older children are generally welcome. Boise and Meridian require registration; the others don't. In Boise, parents must stay with their children; at the others they're generally free to browse in the library.

The **Boise Public Library** offers age-grouped programs for babies through preschoolers in four sessions a year lasting 10 to 12 weeks each. Registration and a library card are required, and popular sessions fill up fast. The library also offers a drop-in story time, drop-in films, and an evening program for kids up to 8. The *Town Square Mall* branch currently has a session Thursday mornings for 3 to 5-year-olds.

The **Garden City Library** weaves magic twice a week during the school year: Tuesday at 10 for ages 3 and up, Wednesdays at 10 for younger children. There's no registration and residence isn't required.

Southwest Ada County is served by the **Ada Community Library** at Victory and Five Mile, with year-round storytelling Tuesdays and Fridays at 10:30. All ages are welcome, there's no registration and parents can browse in the library. There's a branch at the *Star Senior Center* with storytelling on Thursday mornings.

Arts and Crafts

The **Eagle Library** has year-round story sessions Thursdays at 10:30, open to all but geared to preschoolers during school months. No registration is needed and parents can browse in the library.

West Boise and Meridian are served by the **Meridian Library**, with a school-year story program on Thursdays at 10:30 for children 3 to 6. Registration for fall starts in late August, though openings occur throughout the year. Parents can browse in the library.

At Kuna High School, the **Kuna Library** has story hours Wednesdays at 10 and Saturdays at 2 year-round. The sessions are open to all ages, no registration is needed and parents can browse in the library. On the second Thursday of each month during the school year, *Literary Night* draws local authors to read and talk about writing; some, like a recent cowboy poet, have the power to enthrall older children.

All area libraries also have special programs for children and participate in the *Summer Reading Program*, in which students earn small rewards for reading books. All have extensive collections of children's books for borrowing, as well as audio and video tapes and computer programs. Children love to have their own cards, and almost every adventure in this book will be enhanced by a visit to the library!

Music Under the Stars

Boise SummerFest
BSU Centennial Amphitheatre
385-1596

On three weekends in June, **SummerFest** offers music and dance in a lovely little outdoor amphitheatre on the banks of the Boise River. If your children are old enough to sit still for an hour or so, this is a perfect way to introduce them to music.

The series offers vocal and instrumental music in a range of styles, all performed with a light touch in keeping with the setting. Past programs have included show tunes, marches, folk music, big band and jazz, as well as Native American music and ballet.

The second weekend in the series is always reserved for a *Family Concert*, with music sure to appeal to kids. (Songs from *Sesame Street*, perhaps, or the current movie kid-rage.) At that one especially, nobody will mind if your little ones wiggle or if you take them out for a break. There's even a small, slightly-dingy playground behind the Pavilion east of the Amphitheatre, if they need to run and jump!

You'll have to be ready to push their bedtimes, though: the gates open at 7:00 but concerts don't start until 8. (Try using that hour for an al fresco supper.) In 1995, tickets were $8 for adults and $6 for students, with no charge for children under 6. Be sure to bring sweaters.

For information about other events at BSU, call *Select-A-Seat* (385-3535; see p. 28), *ARTSLINE* (376-2787; see pp. 28 and 33) or the appropriate academic department on the BSU campus.

Arts and Crafts

Paint Your Pot

**Ceramica
Pioneer Building
598 W. Main Street
342-3822**

Now *this* is a novel idea! Kids love to play with clay, right? And creating your own masterpiece is wonderfully rewarding. But you can't make pottery from scratch: it takes at lot of know-how you don't have and equipment you can't afford. Enter **Ceramica**, where the hard work is already done and the equipment is there: all you do is decorate!

Here's how it works: You choose your piece from more than a hundred different designs on their shelves; choices range from tiny vegetables and Halloween pumpkins costing a dollar or two to elaborate vases and tea sets that can go as high as $50 or more. For another $6.50 you get glaze, four paints and 90 minutes to work. Extra colors cost $1, extra time goes for $1 for each 15 minutes. They'll give you an instruction sheet, an idea book and all the help you need. Firing is included, and you can usually pick up your finished piece the next day.

If you choose something small, your child should be able to create a finished piece for a total of $10 to $15. Ceramica is open Tuesday through Thursday from 10 to 9, Friday and Saturday from 10 to 10 and on Sunday from noon to 5. Give this one a try!

The Play's the Thing . . .

Idaho Shakespeare Festival
5657 Warm Springs Avenue
336-9221

Though it seems like only yesterday, the **Idaho Shakespeare Festival** is rapidly approaching its 20th birthday. To celebrate, it has moved again -- for the third and, we hope, last time.

The Festival was born downtown in 1977, on the lawn of what is now Angell's restaurant. From the beginning, quality was uniformly high but a permanent home elusive. In 1981 it moved to Plantation Golf Course, in 1985 to land lent by Ore-Ida in ParkCenter. Since the Festival owns its latest home along the river, its fourth site should be permanent.

Performances in the new venue will begin in the summer of 1996. The 600-seat outdoor amphitheater will have improved acoustics and sightlines, built-in tiers and assigned seating; theater-goers will bring chairs. Doors will continue to open an hour early, but whether people will still bring picnics now there's assigned seating remains to be seen.

The best time to take kids -- the *only* time to take little ones -- is *Family Night*, held the Sunday after the opening of each play. Curtain time is at 7 and prices are reduced: In 1995 they were $14.50 for adults and $7.50 for children 6-18. Kids under 6 are free and *only* welcome on Family Nights. Other nights the theater opens at 6:30, with Green Show entertainment at 7:30 and the play at 8. Tickets cost $16.50 for adults and $13.50 for students, with reduced prices for previews of each play.

The real question, of course, is not whether the Bard is ready for your child, but whether your child is ready for the Bard. Shakespearean tragedy is heavy; the comedies are often raucously slapstick, but they're long and the language is hard to follow. Still, if you pick your play carefully, you just may find you have a budding Thespian on your hands.

The Idaho Shakespeare Festival performs four plays each summer; watch for other performances by this talented company, and see p. 100 for a description of their *Halloween haunted house*.

Dance to the Music

Ballet Idaho
516 S. 9th
343-0556

For Boise parents, **Ballet Idaho's** claim to fame is its Christmas production of *The Nutcracker* with the Boise Philharmonic. But that's by no means all this talented company does; indeed, most of its seasons include at least one production suitable for older children.

All performances of Ballet Idaho's fall-to-spring schedule are held in the *Morrison Center* on the Boise State University campus. Tickets are a bit pricey, ranging from $8 to $15 for children and $15 to $30 for adults. Still, the mid-December *Nutcracker,* featuring children from local dance studios, has been close to a sellout for the last few years.

Tickets for all productions are available at *Select-A-Seat* (see p. 28). Ballet Idaho also offers in-school performances and workshops, and teaches dance to children from age 3 through the professional level. Opera fan Joanne Hoyt (see p. 29) is also a dance aficionado; call the Ballet for information about her unique puppet shows.

Other ballet companies around town offer lessons and public performances, many tailored for families and children. Call around if your child wants lessons; watch the newspaper for suitable productions.

Encore!

Idaho Theater for Youth
404 S. 8th St.
345-0060

Have your kids seen a play lately? No? Are you sure about that? If you haven't been searching their backpacks carefully, you may have missed an announcement for an in-school performance by a touring company that's rapidly becoming well-known around the state: 150,000 kids every year see in-school productions of **Idaho Theater for Youth**.

Founded in 1981 and billed as "Idaho's professional theater for young audiences," ITY has performed at the Kennedy Center and was the 1994 recipient of the Governor's Award for Excellence in the Arts. Now you too can see this talented company: in 1995, ITY added public performances to its schedule of school productions and acting classes.

Mainstage currently produces only one play a year but hopes to expand to a full season. Its first production was *Little Lulu;* the 1996 entry is *Charlotte's Web,* which will play for three weeks in May on Stage II at the Morrison Center. Performances will be afternoons and evenings Thursdays through Sundays. Tickets, costing $10 for adults and $7 for children, are available from *Select-A-Seat* (p. 28) or ITY.

ITY offers year-round acting classes for children from 7 on up, with a more intensive program in the summer. Classes are also available through the *Boise Department of Parks and Recreation* (p. 70).

History

Introduction

Many things about raising a child surprised me, among them the fact that whatever developmental timetable I had in my head was sure to be wrong. I didn't imagine a 2-year-old could skip; Kate could. A 4-year-old couldn't ride a bike, I thought; Michael did. And so on. Mostly, they outstripped my imagination -- with one exception: Kate and her friends were all of 6 years old before they had any concept of time.

Turns out that's pretty universal: kids may go to kindergarten knowing their ABC's, able to tie their shoes, even write their names, but few have more than a vague idea of what "today" or "yesterday" mean. (That's why kindergarten teachers spend so much time with clocks, seasons and the calendar!) It follows, then, that exploring "history" is not on most preschoolers' list of fun things to do, and that it is one of the more difficult subjects to impart to children of any age.

What that means for parents is that history is not a "natural" adventure; it must be *made* into one. An extra effort may be needed to make it fun, and whatever learning occurs should be spontaneous. In this area especially, parents should avoid lecturing and questioning. Ask a child, after a ceramics or batik session, what they learned about art and they'll probably be delighted to tell you. Ask that same child what they learned about history, and they may feel like they're being tested.

In this chapter you'll find adventures guaranteed to give kids a hefty dose of fun along with a sense of their heritage. Since children the world over delight in unusual modes of transportation, we start with the *Tour Train*. Then we go way back, to pioneer times which, naturally enough, inspire more curiosity than does the recent past. We'll explore wagon ruts in the desert, visit pioneers from far-off Spain and see Idaho's early history come alive. For older children, there are visits to the *State Capitol*, the *Old Assay Office* and the heart of *Old Boise*, and for all ages, stops at the *Old Penitentiary* and the *Train Depot*.

Here particularly, parents need to be cognizant of a child's age, interests and development level. It won't matter much on the *Tour Train* or at the *Historical Museum*, but not many children under 7 or 8 will get much out of exploring the *Oregon Trail* or touring the *Statehouse*.

✍ ✍ ✍

All Ab-o-o-ard!

Boise Tour Train
Julia Davis Park
342-4796

There's no better way to see the sights of Boise and give kids a thrill at the same time than to take the train! (It's not a real train, of course -- it's a canopied tram pulled by a replica of an 1890's puffer-belly steam engine -- but the absence of tracks only adds to the fun.)

The two-hour tours (over a new route each year) take in some 75 sites, from *Idaho's Statehouse* (p. 47) and the *Idanha Hotel* to the old trolley tracks and historic neighborhoods along *Warm Springs Avenue* and *Harrison Boulevard*. On the way, knowledgeable guides offer a running commentary on architecture, history and famous personalities. Modern Boise isn't neglected either: even natives will pick up fascinating tidbits about *Boise Cascade* and *Morrison Knudsen*, the *Morrison Center* (quick: what shape is the building?), the *BSU Pavilion* and even the blue turf in BSU's *Bronco Stadium*. There are also specialized tours to places like the *Old Pen* (p. 46) and *Idaho City* for groups of 25 or more.

During the summer, the **Boise Tour Train** leaves every hour and fifteen minutes from 10 to 3 Monday through Saturday, and from noon to 5 on Sunday; there's an evening tour at 7 Thursday through Saturday. Call for information about spring and fall schedules.

The Tour Train departs from its own depot at the west end of Julia Davis Park, near the *Idaho Historical Museum (see p. 45)*. There are bathrooms at the museum and in the park, and strollers can be taken on the train or left with attendants at the depot. Tours cost $6 for adults and teens and $3.50 for kids under 12; the toddler crowd rides free.

With the possible exception of teens (who knows about *them*?), kids of any age will get a kick out of this ride. And it's safe for even the youngest, as long as you hold them in your lap.

Along the Dusty Trail

Oregon Trail
Ada and Elmore Counties

In just two decades, between 1841 and 1861, more than 300,000 Americans came west on the **Oregon Trail**. The trail stretched 2,000 miles from Independence, Missouri, to present-day Oregon City and included more than 1,700 miles of trails and cutoffs in southern Idaho. Happily, the remnants of almost 600 miles can still be seen today, and many are within a short drive from the capital city.

Stop first at the *Idaho State Historical Museum* (p. 45) to pick up a map and look at artifacts, and at the *library* (p. 34) to check out a children's book on westward expansion. Then head for *Bonneville Point*, where the pioneers traveling with Captain Bonneville in 1833 had their first look at the Boise Valley. Take I-84 east to Exit 64 (Blacks Creek/Kuna-Mora Road) and turn left (northeast) on Blacks Creek Road. It's about four miles to the historical marker at Bonneville Point, where you can explore the nearby wagon ruts.

Get back on I-84 and head east toward Mountain Home. Take Exit 95 (Fairfield-Sun Valley) and follow U.S. 20 northeast about six miles, turning right on Hot Springs Road. (If you reach the Rattlesnake Station Historical Site you've gone too far.) Follow Hot Springs about a mile to *Teapot Dome*, a landmark on the Oregon Trail. The trail passes the bottom of the dome, and you can hike up for an excellent view.

Now get back on U.S. 20 and continue northeast three more miles to *Emigrant Road* on the left, just before Tollgate. Emigrant follows the Oregon Trail for about 25 miles, turning into Foothills and Mayfield before it brings you back to Blacks Creek. There are several places you can park and explore; just don't trespass on private property.

Allow half a day for this adventure. Wear layered clothes and sturdy shoes, avoid hot days and don't forget water and sunblock. To witness a re-enactment of an *Oregon Trail river crossing*, see p. 95. And consider visiting the *Oregon Trail Interpretive Center* in Baker, Oregon.

History

It's History!

Idaho State Historical Museum
610 N. Julia Davis Dr.
334-2120

From Lewis and Clark and the Oregon Trail to Chinese herbs and the story of Idaho's strange boundaries, the Gem State's colorful past comes to life at the **Idaho State Historical Museum**.

Small children will bypass many exhibits, but there's still much to delight them, especially re-creations of a saloon, a bank, a blacksmith's shop, a 1930's kitchen and the aforementioned Chinese herb shop. Imaginative preschoolers will delight, too, in the stories of Idaho's more colorful characters -- Diamondfield Jack, Polly Bemis, Jim Bridger.

On the last Saturday in September the *Museum Comes to Life*, with dedicated volunteers portraying Idaho pioneers. Kids are more than spectators at this event: they get to try out old-time crafts and even do some chores the pioneer way (that *ought* to show them how easy they've got it, but of course it won't.) Don't miss this one!

On the museum's lower floor, objects from its permanent collection tell the story of Idaho from prehistoric times through the fur traders, gold-seekers and early pioneers, with stops at the state's Native American, Basque and Chinese heritage.

On the grounds, the Historical Society also operates a small pioneer village containing two 1860's log cabins, an adobe house from 1865 that belonged to the town's four-term mayor, and a simple frame house typical of the late 1800's. East of town, on Warm Springs Avenue, the Society offers a small museum and self-guided tours of Idaho's fascinating *Old Territorial Penitentiary* (p. 46).

The museum is open Monday through Saturday from 9 to 5, Sundays and holidays 1 to 5. Admission is free but donations are requested. For gifts that say "Idaho," check the shop on the main floor.

✍ ✍ ✍

Bars and Stripes

Old Idaho Penitentiary
2445 E. Old Penitentiary Road
368-6080

It's not for everyone -- indeed, sensitive children may find it disturbing -- but for many families, a visit to Idaho's **Old Territorial Penitentiary** can be a enlightening way to spend an afternoon.

Once you've seen it you'll find it hard to believe that prisoners were housed there until 1974, when the new prison was opened south of Gowen Field. (The most famous inmate was Harry Orchard, confessed killer of Gov. Frank Steunenberg. He was held for almost 50 years until his death in 1954.) The first cellhouse in the Old Pen was built in 1870, less than ten years after Idaho became a territory. Over the years it grew into a complex of buildings, many built by the prisoners themselves from stone quarried nearby and cut into blocks by hand.

Get a map and begin your self-guided tour at the small museum, where you'll find portraits of famous inmates, stories of crime and punishment and views of the prison in territorial times. You can see an 18-minute slide show and visit the Warden's Office and Women's Ward. On the grounds you'll get a look at the institutional architecture of the day. (The prison is listed on the National Register of Historic Places.) You can visit cellhouses, view the effects of a riot and enter a row of solitary punishment cells known as "Siberia." If you want, you can visit Death Row and its gallows area. Incongruously, there are also interesting exhibits on the history of electricity and transportation, the latter including a 1903 steam fire pump truck and a stagecoach.

The Old Pen is open seven days a week from 10 to 6 Memorial Day through Labor Day, noon to 5 the rest of the year. Admission is $3 for adults, $2 for children 6-12. Wear old clothes and walking shoes!

Other historic buildings include the *Old Assay Office* (p. 49), the *Egyptian Theater* (pp. 50, 82), the *Train Depot* (p. 51) and the French Chateau-style *Idanha Hotel* at 10th and Main, which has housed such notables as Teddy Roosevelt, Ethel Barrymore and Clarence Darrow.

It's the Law

Idaho Statehouse
Capitol and Jefferson
334-2000 (January - March)

Each January, lawmakers from around Idaho gather to decide what the state will spend, who can make your dentures, what the penalty for poaching will be, and a thousand other things that affect your life.

We're fortunate to have one of the most accessible governments in the nation. You can visit the governor's office, watch legislators debate and see where the Supreme Court used to meet. The governor himself might even stop to greet you!

Idaho's **Statehouse** was modeled after the U.S. Capitol in Washington, D.C. Its neo-classical center was built between 1905 and 1912 from sandstone quarried by inmates at Table Rock; the east and west wings were added in 1919 to accommodate the House and Senate. The building's granite base was shipped from Vermont; the eagle atop the dome is bronze-plated copper. The columns inside are Corinthian, the floors rock maple, the woodwork mahogany. The multi-colored marbles came from as far away as Italy, but the columns aren't marble at all: their veneer is a mix of gypsum, glue, marble dust and granite!

The only statehouse in the nation heated geothermally is open from 7 a.m. to 6 p.m. weekdays and from 9 to 5 on weekends, but it's at its best during legislative sessions. Most mornings and early afternoons, you can watch lawmakers in action from one of the 4th floor galleries. In the morning you may also see the legislature's budget committee, but in any case don't miss their meeting room: it was the original chambers of the Idaho Supreme Court. And check Idaho's flag, featuring the only state seal designed by a woman (Emma Edwards Green).

To start your tour, step to the center of the rotunda on the ground floor and look up: 43 stars in a sky-blue background represent Idaho's entry into the union as the 43rd state. The miner's statue nearby commemorates 91 miners who died in the 1972 Sunshine Mine disaster; the symbols on the sundial represent Idaho's major industries; the scale model of the Capitol Mall includes both present and planned buildings.

Then stroll the east and west hallways, where changing displays depict life in Idaho: its agriculture, fish and wildlife, timber, water and geology. Check the gemstone display, which includes Idaho's official state gem, the star garnet; and the huge section of White Pine, whose dateline gives you an eerie feel for the life of a tree: it was already pretty big when the Declaration of Independence was signed!

In the 2nd floor rotunda you'll find a replica of "Winged Victory" (a gift from the French) and a fascinating equestrian statue of George Washington carved from a yellow pine tree! Head down the west wing to the Governor's office, east to the offices of other state officials.

Your main stop on the 3rd floor is the former home of the Idaho Supreme Court, now the meeting room of the legislature's budget committee. There's an information booth on this floor from January through March. If they're not in session, you can visit the House and Senate floors; otherwise, watch from one of the 4th floor galleries. On the 4th floor, examine the series of murals called "Legend of Dreams," commemorating people and places who have shaped life in Idaho.

Take a break now, for a picnic on the lovely lawn. That's a replica of the Liberty Bell at the bottom of the main steps; across the street is the Steunenberg Statue, honoring the assassinated governor. (Check out a book from the library for more on this fascinating case.) *Capitol Park*, surrounding the monument, is a nice shady spot. There's a Civil War cannon at the southwest corner of the Statehouse; the Tree of Guernica on the west lawn, brought over from the Basque Country in 1981; the Pioneer Monument on the southeast corner; and the Grand Army of the Republic Monument near the west entrance.

To the east lies the *Ada County Courthouse*, a 1930's WPA project in art deco style. Further east are the *Supreme Court* and *State Library*. Just north are the *Len B. Jordan* and *Joe R. Williams State Office Buildings*. The *Old Federal Building and Post Office* is a block south, the new *Federal Building* four blocks north on Fort Street.

Assay This!

Old Assay Office
Main and 2nd
334-3861

This 1872 building is nothing more or less than an oversized vault. Inside its two-foot-thick walls and barred windows, about $75 million in gold passed through the hands of its assayers: a tribute to the importance of mining in Idaho's early history.

Built by the federal government at a cost of $73,000, the initial task of the **Old Assay Office** was simply to value gold and silver so miners could price their product; this was done by determining the percentage of the precious metals in selected samples. By the late 1880's, though, the office had begun buying high-quality gold which it melted, refined into bars and shipped to a mint for coinage.

In the early years of the 20th century, mining began a steady decline. The Assay Office was closed in 1933, along with similar offices in Helena and Salt Lake City and the mint at Carson City, Nevada.

Today the sandstone structure is a National Historic Landmark, occupied by state offices. It's been altered a bit: windows were added to the rear wall in the 1930's, and more recently the bars on the second floor windows were removed. But it's still an impressive building and an excellent reminder of Idaho's early history.

The building is owned by the *Idaho State Historical Society*; the ground floor is open to visitors free of charge during business hours.

Heart of the City

Old Boise
Main & Idaho
5th to 8th Streets

A relaxed stroll through historic **Old Boise**, with frequent stops to nibble and discover, can be an exhilarating adventure for both parent and child. Get your urban adventure off to a fitting start by taking the bus. (Call 336-1010 for times and routes.) Just remember that they often run only once an hour and plan accordingly.

Leave the bus on Idaho near 8th. Head south a block and left on Main, stopping to let the kids do cartwheels on the lawn of the *WestOne Plaza*. (The tallest building in Boise, it features an exhibit of banking history.) At the corner of Capitol, check the restored *Egyptian Theater*, replete with brightly-painted lotus columns, statues and hieroglyphics typical of the architectural fad triggered by the discovery of King Tut's tomb in the 1920's. For a closer look, see p. 82.

Catty-corner from the Egyptian is the *Perrault Building*, the area's oldest surviving commercial structure. Continue east past the *Empire Theater* (movies cost a nickel in 1904), *Masonic Hall*, *Telephone* and *Statesman* buildings. Stop to check the fossils at *Walkabout Creek* and crane your neck at the prancing horse atop the *Pioneer Tent Building*.

A block south on 6th is the *Basque Museum* (p. 52), well worth a visit now or later. Continue east past the lovely brick *Turnverein* and two-story *Spiegle* buildings. At the corner of 5th is the massive medieval *Belgravia* -- once the most desirable apartment house in Boise.

For a break, turn south a few steps to *C.W. Moore Park*, a peaceful, historic urban oasis complete with stream and waterwheel. The magnolias are lovely in spring and their petals make wonderful boats. (Remember "Pooh Sticks"?) You can unpack your picnic or carry something out from one of the distinctive eateries in the neighborhood.

After lunch head back up 5th, across Idaho and left past the old *Star Boarding House* and the historic *Central Fire Station*. Across the street are two Victorian townhouses; at the corner of Capitol stands the brick *Adelmann Building*. Turn left, cross Idaho again and spend a few

History 51

minutes visiting the *City-County Building*, which houses Boise's City Council. The bubbling fountain in the courtyard is always a draw.

You're almost back where you started, but before you catch the bus stroll down 8th to the *Grove*, where you can end your urban jaunt playing in the *fountain* (p. 113) and examining the statuary.

✍ ✍ ✍

Train Lore

Union Pacific Train Depot
2603 Eastover Terrace
386-7500

Fascinated by trains? Want a taste of Boise's past? Just looking for a cool spot on a hot afternoon? Try the **Union Pacific Train Depot** at the south end of Capitol Boulevard.

The depot has known its share of change. Built in 1925, it marked the successful end of a 50-year campaign to bring the railroad to Boise. It served that purpose until 1971, when Union Pacific dropped its passenger service. Amtrak came along in the 80's and passenger trains again rolled in, but they used little of the cavernous old depot. It was bought by the Morrison Knudsen Corporation in 1990 and beautifully renovated for office space and a railroad museum; as we go to press the city and private citizens are trying to raise money to buy it from MK.

The Mission-style depot, which is on the National Register of Historic Places, is currently open from 10 to 4 Monday through Friday, and closed on weekends and holidays. Admission is $3 for adults, $2 for college students and $1 for children 6 to 18. You can stroll the lovely grounds free of charge at any time.

You'll have no trouble getting *to* the depot: just make a right on Eastover as Capitol winds up the hill. Getting back to town is another matter, however: your best bet is to take a right on Crescent Rim, a right on Capitol and find a place to turn around. If the depot is to return to its rightful place in the community, the egress problem must be addressed.

✍ ✍ ✍

Basque in It

Basque Museum and Cultural Center
607 & 611 Grove St.
343-2671

Boise is the center of one of the largest Basque populations outside of Spain, yet many Idahoans know little of their history. The **Basque Museum and Cultural Center** will fill you in.

The parents and grandparents of Idaho's Basques came primarily from the Bizhaia region in the Pyrenees Mountains in northern Spain, recruited in the late 19th century to work as sheepherders. Basques are considered the oldest ethnic group in Europe, and have preserved their ancient language, customs and traditions since Paleolithic times. The "Basque Country" was granted regional autonomy in 1980, but many Basques continue to press for full independence.

The Basque Museum is housed in an old home next to the historic *Basque Sheepherder's Boarding House*. (Many Basque men, single or with wives back home, lived in such houses.) The two buildings hold furnishings and exhibits depicting the Basque experience in Idaho and the contributions they've made to government, education and the arts. For kids, there's an interactive exhibit in which Basque instruments play traditional music in response to the push of a button.

The museum is open Tuesday through Friday from 10 to 4 and Saturday from 11 to 3. Admission is free, but donations are welcome.

To round out the experience, follow your museum visit with lunch or dinner at *Basque Onati*, in the Ranch Club at Orchard and Chinden, or *Bar Guernika*, 202 S. Capitol Boulevard. Watch the newspaper for performances by the exciting *Oinkari Basque Dancers* and for the *Basque Jaialdi* (festival), held every five years in Boise.

Sports and Recreation

Introduction

If you've lived in the Treasure Valley for more than a day and a half, it will come as no surprise to you that it's a sporting paradise. Boiseans practically *live* outdoors most of the year: running, jogging and 'blading the Greenbelt, biking the Boise Front, tubing the river, skiing at Bogus. There's hiking in every direction, and more places to swim than you can shake the proverbial stick at.

Physical activity keeps kids strong and healthy, builds their self-esteem and keeps them out of trouble. The challenge for parents is to tailor the opportunities that exist to the interests, abilities and attention span of their offspring. That isn't always easy, as anyone can tell you whose 6-year-old has been knocked off her bike by a speeding 'blader, who's taken a child on the river only to dump the raft, or spent two hours getting ready to go skiing only to have the kid announce that she's *cold*.

In this chapter you'll find a set of recipes for enjoying the out-of-doors with children of all ages. The old standards are here -- from tubing the Boise and skiing Shafer Butte to riding the 'tube and coasting at Camel's Back -- but you'll find some new twists as well: scaling a faux-rock wall, horseback riding in the Boise Front, piloting a raft a la Huck Finn. Throughout this chapter, safety is a foremost consideration: you'll find out why many parents set age limits for floating the river, why Camel's Back can be a dangerous place to coast, and what to watch out for at Eagle Island and Sandy Point.

Spectator sports are touched on only lightly here. In addition to *Hawks* baseball, I recommend any of the minor sports at *BSU* and, for older children or avid bikers, the *PowerBar International Women's Challenge*. You may also enjoy horse racing at Les Bois Park; as racetracks go, it's pretty kid-friendly. And we've had some great spontaneous adventures at local high schools, watching their teams practice. Pole vaulting up close is *very* impressive!

Organized sports are beyond the scope of this book, but parents should be aware that popular team games like soccer fill up fast. Call the appropriate entity *well in advance* to avoid disappointment.

✿ ❄ ✿

Sports and Recreation

Down the Tube!

Natatorium
1811 Warm Springs
345-9270

Take Boise's only toddler pool, add reasonably warm water and the best water slide in town, and you've got the **Natatorium**.

Located behind Adams School at the end of the old Warm Springs Avenue trolley line, Boise's premiere public swimming pool takes its name from the original Natatorium, a graceful four-story Victorian swimming pool-cum-dance hall, torn down in 1934 because of wind damage. When the Nat was built in 1892 you could have a swim, complete with suit, towel and dressing room, for 25 cents!

We were first drawn to the Nat by its lovely toddler pool, sloping gently to a depth of 18" and featuring spouting seals and a mushroom fountain. (The "deep" end is just right for brand-new swimmers.) And the hydrotube was always a draw. But what has brought us back time and again is the Nat's water temperature, warmed by a combination of geothermal energy and a conventional heater. At 80 degrees it's no bathtub, but *lots* warmer than the liquid ice in the city's other pools!

The Nat's main pool is undistinguished and often crowded, but it does have two diving boards. Children are generally around 5 before they can stand in the shallow end, and since flotation devices are banned, the pool isn't much use to families before that. Kids must be able to swim across and back before they can go in the deep end.

The fully-enclosed hydrotube is fairly gentle by water slide standards, with a splashdown system someone should patent: you're deposited in the deep end of a heated pool, where the force of the water carries you effortlessly to the steps at the shallow end; instead of having to somehow stand up while still clutching your toddler, you simply support the youngster as both of you are propelled to safety. And if you put one of the free tubes on your child, even that support is effortless. Naturally, parents should test the slide before taking children with them.

(As a parent, I'm grateful for such an ingenious system. As a grownup, I must admit that the Hydrotube's *real* attraction for me is it's steamy sub-tropical feel; every time I ride I give silent thanks to my daughter for providing me the "cover" to do such childish things!)

The Nat's dressing rooms are clean but unappealing, with two showers but no private changing rooms. Water often puddles on the floor, so parents should insist on deck shoes. Sadly, the attractive, well-staffed snack bar offers virtually nothing of much nutritional value, so bring your own. You can eat on the deck or grass, but not poolside.

One drawback to all city pools are the rules, which are unevenly enforced and sometimes seem capricious. (Non-swimmers can't sit with you, for instance, unless they don bathing suits; that can make it hard to bring elderly relatives.) Another is the lack of chairs -- on a hot summer's day you'll be unlikely to find one. The grounds are lovely though, and if your kids don't have to be watched every minute you can spread a blanket on the cool grass and take a snooze or read a book.

All city pools open the last day of school for free swimming, and close when schools re-open in late August or early September. Daytime swimming costs $2.50 for adults, $1.75 for teens and $1.25 for children under 12; evening swims are $.75 - $1.50, and there's a $5 Sunday family swim as well as season and half-season passes. Slide rides cost $5 for 10 or $6 for an all day pass (but remember that rides left from your 10 can be used another day; the passes can't). Pools are open daily from 1:30 to 5:30 and Monday through Saturday evenings 7 to 9.

Swimming lessons are offered in two-week half-hour sessions, Monday through Thursday from 9 to 11:30 and 5:30 to 6:30. (Evening classes fill fast!) They cost $20 and instruction follows the American Red Cross *Learn to Swim* program. Registration is in late May; kids then attend a screening session and are assigned to classes based on skill. (We chose the Nat because they teach in the warm splashdown pool -- meaning I heard no complaints on cool mornings!) Each pool has a swim team, water aerobics, adult lessons and Friday night teen parties.

The other city pools are *Borah*, at 801 Aurora (375-8373), *Fairmont*, at 7929 Northview (375-3011), *Lowell*, at 1601 N. 28th St. (345-7918) and *South*, at 921 Shoshone (345-1984). You can swim at the *Y* with a membership or day pass (344-5501) or at *BSU* if you're a student, a staff member or a member of the faculty.

✧ ✧ ✧

Sports and Recreation

Islands in the Sun

**Eagle Island State Park
Hatchery Road
Eagle
939-0696 (Summer)
939-0704 (Winter)**

Pools are great, but sometimes kids just *have* to play in the sand. And sometimes you just *have* to lie in the sun and read a good book. Happily, there are two excellent beaches both within minutes of Boise.

Our top choice is **Eagle Island State Park**, for its warmer water and great hydrotube. But be warned: lifeguards were sacrificed to budget cuts in 1995 and swimming is no longer officially recommended, so you're on your own. The slope is gentle but the water gets deep, so check it out carefully before you take your eyes off the kids. Shade can be hard to come by here too; be an early bird or bring an umbrella.

Pack bathing suits, towels, snacks, sunblock, rafts, tubes, toys and that book you've been dying to read (but no pets or glass containers) and head west through Eagle on State Street (Highway 44). Turn left on Linder Road and left on Hatchery. Or take Chinden Boulevard, turning right at Linder and right on Hatchery. There are signs to the park.

Eagle Island lies between the north and south channels of the Boise River and was originally a prison farm. The small island in the middle of the swimming area is man-made in the shape of an eagle. (Honest!) There are barbecue pits, picnic tables, and a concession stand open from noon to 6. The bathrooms and changing rooms are clean and pleasant, but the only showers are in the waterslide area.

The waterslide is open from noon to 8 and has lifeguards. Try it *without* a mat first for a slower ride, and take kids before sending them alone. Ten rides cost $3 and can be shared; an all-day non-transferable pass is $6. Eagle Island is open from 10:30 a.m. to 9:30 p.m. Memorial Day through Labor Day, closed the rest of the year. Admission is $2 a carload; see p. 58 for information about season passes to all state parks.

✧ ✧ ✧

Islands in the Sun II

Sandy Point
Lucky Peak State Park
Highway 21
344-0240

Sandy Point is even more popular than *Eagle Island*, in part because you can get there on bikes (see p. 62; it's too long a ride for small children). Driving, head southeast nine miles via Warm Springs Avenue and Idaho 21; turn left at the sign just below Lucky Peak Dam.

The place lives up to its name admirably, with an attractive sandy beach and lots of shade. But the water is colder than at Eagle Island (p. 57), and it too lost its lost its lifeguards in 1995. The popular fountain is still there but the roped-off swimming area is gone: until money for the lifeguards is restored, you're on your own.

Sandy Point is part of *Lucky Peak State Park*. It has bathrooms, changing rooms and even an outside shower for rinsing off all that sand. There's plenty of room to picnic or barbecue and a fairly extensive selection at the concession stand, open from 11 to 4:30. There's fishing and boating at nearby *Discovery State Park* and *Lucky Peak Marina*.

The park itself is open from 7 a.m. to 9 p.m. Memorial Day through Labor Day, 7 to 4 the rest of the year. Admission is $2 a carload. Season passes good at all state parks cost $15 if purchased between January and March, $25 the rest of the year. They're available at the *Idaho Department of Parks and Recreation* (5657 Warm Springs Avenue; 334-4199) or at any state park when attendants are present.

If you like ice-cold water, you can also swim at *Lucky Peak Reservoir*, there's a nice little beach near Grimes Creek. In Canyon County, try *Lake Lowell*, southwest of Nampa.

☼ ☼ ☼

Sports and Recreation

It's Tubular!

Boise River
Barber Park
Ann Morrison Park

'Tubing the Boise' is the quintessential summertime adventure, but remember that it's not a theme park: it's a real river, and kids *have* drowned. So take a few common-sense precautions: wait 'til the experts declare the river floatable, try it alone before you take the kids, never take small children (use your judgement; my personal limit is 7), put life jackets on *everyone* (yours will help you rescue a child if you have to) and *don't drink*. If you do those things, you can relax and enjoy.

The most popular float begins at *Barber Park* east of Boise and ends eight miles downstream at *Ann Morrison*. It takes two to three hours depending on current, and "popular" is an understatement: don't go on a weekend unless you like crowds. Watch the newspaper to see when it's safe to float (usually early July but sometimes later) and start by early afternoon: the river cools off fast once it's in shadow.

You can rent rafts, tubes and life jackets (with crotch straps) at *Wheels R Fun* (see p. 67), *Barber Park* (they won't rent to kids weighing less than 50 lbs., which should tell you something), some sporting goods stores or through the *BSU Outdoor Rental Center*, or buy them at tire stores, auto parts dealers or sporting goods stores. Don't buy a cheap raft; the rocks you're sure to scrape will destroy it.

Rafts are mandatory for small children. With older ones, the choice is personal: tubes are more maneuverable, but small bottoms get cold and it's hard to stay together; a raft will keep you dryer, but you have to get the hang of it -- couples have been known to come to blows over how to steer. You can also tie tubes together, which solves the problem of scary separations but cuts down on maneuverability.

Wear old shorts, t-shirts and *shoes*. Take food, water (no glass, please), sunglasses and sunblock in a waterproof bag, sweatshirts, towels and more snacks in a second bag for after. Except on weekends when lines are long, don't inflate your tubes; there's air at Barber Park.

Your best bet is to park at Barber ($2) and send one person back there on the shuttle after the float (another $2). Shuttles run every hour and you can take them both ways but you'll spend money and time. To avoid the shuttle altogether you'll need two cars. Put your "after" bag in Car 1, *along with a key to Car 2*, and leave Car 1 (locked) near the footbridge in Ann Morrison Park. Put your float bag, tubes and life jackets in Car 2, *a key to Car 1 in someone's zip pocket*, and head out Warm Springs Avenue to Eckert Road. Barber is a quarter-mile south.

Launching can be tricky: watch others, and be prepared to get wet. Once on the river, *stay in the middle*: the real hazard isn't rocks or even the tiny waterfalls; it's the overhanging tree branches on the banks. In a raft, keep in mind that *people paddling opposite ways on opposite sides will go nowhere*; let one adult steer while the other stands ready to help. When there's a choice of stream channel, go where others go.

This is no wilderness float, but it's lovely all the same -- largely because of the trees that will knock you off if you get careless! At first you'll pass a few buildings, irrigation pumps and the remains of a lumber yard; after *Memorial Park* you'll float by *Morrison Knudsen*, *Boise State University*, the *Morrison Center* and three city parks. Along the way you'll see joggers and bikers on the *Greenbelt*, fish in the river and herons in the air. You might even see a muskrat. Just watch out for 'boarders at the bridge pylons, and mischievous kids up above.

The float goes over three small "waterfalls;" you'll hear them before you see them, and you may want to portage small children around them. In a raft, put kids on the floor, hang on, and steer where everyone else is going. In tubes, send an adult first and have them beach to wait for the kids. It's a good time for a break, to have a picnic lunch or just let adults rest while the kids play along the river bank.

You'll probably spend the first half of the float being nervous, the second half wishing it wouldn't end. But when you see the footbridge in Ann Morrison Park it's time to beach; there's a *real* waterfall just beyond the park boundary. Grab your "after" bag from the car, dry off, deflate your tubes, head back to Barber and make plans to do it all again. For two quite different floats, see pages 61 and 120.

✧ ✧ ✧

It's Tubular! II

Boise River
Glenwood to Star
Star to Middleton

Don't attempt this less-urbanized adventure until you've mastered the *Barber-to-Boise* part of the river (see p. 59).

There are 64 miles of the **Boise River** from *Lucky Peak* to its confluence with the *Snake*, and most of them are navigable if you have good directions and are willing to portage occasionally. (Parts of the *Payette* can also be rafted by beginners and children; see p. 120.)

You'll need two cars for this float, since there are no shuttles. Take Highway 44 (State Street) through Eagle to *Star*, make a left on Star Road and leave Car 1 at the bridge (in *Middleton* for a longer trip). Take Car 2 back to *Glenwood* and launch from the rocky beach just west of the bridge. Between Glenwood and the bridge at Eagle Road you'll float through the fancy homes and gorgeous yards of *Riverside Village*. At the fork just beyond Riverside, marked by old bridge tailings, *stay to the left* -- the right fork has several small dams.

Between Eagle and Linder Roads you'll pass picnic benches, a rope just made for swinging, and evidence of the river's beaver population. Just before Linder, you'll need to *beach on the right* and carry your raft about 50 yards around Phyllis Canal. At Linder Road, the right fork joins back up for a trip through farm country, interspersed with expensive hillside homes to remind you of Boise's growth. The junk cars you see along the banks were an early form of erosion control.

You can end your trip at *Star Bridge*, or portage around a small dam and continue on to *Middleton*, through a narrow stretch of river rife with reeds and waterfowl. A pleasant way to spend a lazy afternoon!

✡ ✡ ✡

Wheels

Boise River Greenbelt
384-4240

Bikes are to the elementary set what cars are to high schoolers: a symbol of freedom and independence, a chance to venture beyond the watchful eye of parents. If you ride with them when they're young, show them the terrain and teach them the rules of the road, they'll be ready to try their wings safely and happily.

The **Boise River Greenbelt** is ideal for family riding: smooth, shady and close to everything. But it's also ideal for serious bikers, walkers, joggers, skaters and just about everyone else, so until your kids are comfortable on their bikes and familiar with the territory, take them during working hours or early on weekend mornings. During the evening and weekend "rush hours" a skater speeding by or a biker yelling "on your left" is all too likely to cause a fall.

The 15-mile paved path runs from *Willow Lane Athletic Complex* off State Street east to *Discovery State Park* near Lucky Peak, traversing seven parks, *Boise State University* and *Warm Springs Golf Course*. In its "urban" stretch -- between *Kathryn Albertson* and *Municipal* parks -- the Greenbelt is actually two paths most of the way, one on each side of the river, with bridges in *Ann Morrison* and *Julia Davis*.

There are two schools of thought about where to take kids. One says the amenities along the Greenbelt's urban stretch make it the most suitable; the other favors the less crowded sections west of Kathryn Albertson and east of Municipal. Like true fence-sitters we subscribe to both theories, depending on circumstance: if we ride on a Sunday afternoon we head east or west; the rest of the time we stick to the middle, where playgrounds and ice cream cones abound.

Pick up a map from the Parks Department, and make sure you and the kids have properly-sized bikes and snug-fitting helmets. You can rent them at a bike shop or at *Wheels R Fun*, near 13th Street on the Greenbelt (343-8228; see p. 67). Pack water, a pump and a patch kit and you're on your way. Try parking away from the epicenter -- at Municipal Park, near the 13th Street Post Office or at Willow Lane.

Sports and Recreation

For your first ride, make use of the half-mile markers: pedal one marker east and back, then one marker west and back. That way you'll get a two-mile ride without straying far from where you started. After you've done that a time or two, you're ready to explore.

Head east from Willow Lane over a wooden bridge and under the parkway to Veterans Park. (The bridge to your left takes a short loop around a pond.) There are restrooms near the bridge as you leave Veterans, passing under Main and Fairview, through Riverside Park and under Americana. *To avoid crossing Capitol Boulevard, take the footbridge into Ann Morrison Park* and follow the tunnels under 9th and Capitol to BSU. At the footbridge, cross into Julia Davis and head east under Broadway to Municipal. At the junction bear right to Warm Springs Golf Course and the end of the Greenbelt at Discovery State Park.

The Greenbelt's urban stretch has endless places to stop and rest, or do something for a change of pace. The playground in *Ann Morrison Park* makes a nice break, as does a round of *miniature golf* (p. 110) or a *boat ride* (p. 106) in Julia Davis. You can also visit the *MK Nature Center* (p. 7), *Zoo Boise* (p. 10), the *Discovery Center* (p. 6), the *Boise Art Museum* (p. 30) or the *Idaho State Historical Museum* (p. 45).

✧ ✧ ✧

Climb Every Mountain

| Military Reserve Park | Hull's Gulch | Boise Ridge Road |
| Mountain Cove Rd. | 8th St. Extension | Bogus Basin Road |

The **Boise Front** is mountain bike heaven; with a few precautions even the youngest rider can grab a piece of the action.

First be sure each kid has a properly fitted bike and helmet (adults too). Grab a water bottle, a tire pump and a patch kit and you're on your way. Start out close to home in **Military Reserve Park**. From Reserve Street take Mountain Cove Road to any of a number of pullouts and explore the park's bike trails and dirt roads. For a steeper ride, try **Hull's Gulch**. Head north on 8th Street until the pavement ends; continue on 8th Street Extension. The dirt road climbs gently for about a mile, hits a short rugged section, then continues north; it's 3.3 miles to the Hulls Gulch Interpretive Trail lower trailhead, six miles to the upper trailhead (see p. 65) and 7.8 miles to the BLM gate at Boise Ridge Road.

For an exciting downhill ride, approach **Ridge Road** from the north. Drive about 13 miles up Bogus Basin Road until you see a couple of red and blue posts on your right. Ride east down the dirt road; after about two miles you'll hook into the *Bogus-to-Boise trail*. It's 15 downhill miles from there to Camel's Back Park or the end of 8th St.

A big hill on *Cartwright Road* starts some good rides through rolling terrain. Start at the LDS Church at Cartwright and Bogus Basin; after 3.5 miles turn left on Pierce Park and loop back to Hill Road, or stay on Cartwright, left at Dry Creek and straight on Seaman Gulch.

You can mix exercise and spectacular views at *Mores Mountain*, near Shafer Butte (see p. 65). And once your kids are good riders, they'll get a thrill out of the chair lifts at *Bogus Basin Ski Resort* (see p. 72). Three or four Saturdays a summer, you can ride all day and bike back down for $12. The terrain ranges from experienced beginner to expert; Bogus has repair and rental facilities as well as food and music.

✧ ✧ ✧

Sports and Recreation

Take a Hike!

Hulls Gulch Trail
8th Street Extension

Birds of Prey Natural Area
South of Kuna

Deer Flat National Wildlife Refuge
Southwest of Nampa

Mores Mountain
Bogus Basin Road

They're never too young to hit the trail -- though sometimes *you* may feel too old. Boise is a walker's paradise, but it takes a bit of searching to find hikes small children can handle.

Before you head out, dress the kids in comfortable shoes and layered clothes and pack plenty of high-energy food and water. A bag for their "treasures" is a great idea, along with nature books, fanny packs, hats and sunscreen. If you're venturing any distance, you'll also want a map, flashlight, first aid kit and mosquito repellent. If you can find an adult strong enough to carry a little one, take them too!

Ease into it slowly, starting with the trails in *Military Reserve* or *Kathryn Albertson Park*. Then head up 8th Street Extension to **Hulls Gulch** -- Boise's best-known and most crowded urban trail. It's three miles from the end of the pavement to the lower trailhead, another three to the upper. The upper makes a 2.5 mile loop, or you can retrace your steps on the lower. They do connect, but to do that you'll need two cars or someone willing to hike back. Watch out for stickery plants lurking just off the trail, and don't let your kids put *anything* in their mouths.

For scenery, you can't beat **Mores Mountain**, an easy two to four-mile hike near *Bogus Basin Ski Resort*. Head up Bogus Basin Road 16 miles to the ski area; drive through the parking lot and stay to the left, following signs to the Nordic trailhead. After you go through the gate and past the ski hut, it's 3.6 miles on Forest Service 374 to the right-hand turnoff for Shafer Butte Picnic Area. Drive 1.7 miles on *narrow, winding* FS 366 to the picnic area. Eat lunch surrounded by spectacular views of the Boise Valley to the south and the Sawtooth Mountains to the north. Try June for wildflowers, October for the yellow aspens and August as a welcome break from the stifling heat of the valley below

The shortest loop, only a mile, is a signed nature trail with good views in both directions. For a longer hike, take a left at the fork and go on to the summit; it's about a mile round-trip from there, with an altitude gain of 540 feet. The rock outcropping to the west has a great view.

This is a popular, well-developed area with plenty of tables and benches, indoor chemical toilets, water in the summer and a paved section with a short trail and special tables accessible to wheelchairs.

The **Birds of Prey Natural Area** houses the densest concentration of these birds in North America, plus a scenic hike though sage and lava rock. Beware of summer here, though: it can be *very* hot. Take Exit 44 off I-84 and follow Idaho 69 south to Kuna, then Swan Falls Road 17 miles south to the canyon's edge. Park by the dam and walk through the gate. The trail begins as a road, becoming a trail after 1.5 miles as it passes below 300-foot black cliffs. It's another mile to the trail's end and a great view of *Castle Butte*.

In Canyon County, try **Deer Flat National Wildlife Refuge**, on the shores of Lake Lowell southwest of Nampa. Take I-84 west to Exit 36 and follow the signs through Nampa to Highway 45 (12th Avenue South). Take 45 south to Lake Lowell Avenue, turn right and follow it to the end. The Visitors Center has a short nature hike, a "kid's space" with nature-related activities, and children's programs in the evening. You can also use maintenance roads to hike along the lake starting at *Gotts Point*.

✧ ✧ ✧

Sports and Recreation

Get in Line . . .

**Boise River Greenbelt
384-4240**

Unless your kids are dyed-in-the-wool traditionalists, roller skating for them means *roller blading*: wheels in line instead of in pairs. Adults may find it daunting, but most kids take to "blading" like ducks to water.

Happily, Boise is blessed with great places to blade, most notably the **Boise River Greenbelt**. For your first try, rent -- don't buy -- skates at a sporting goods store or at *Wheels R Fun* on the Greenbelt at 13th Street near the Post Office (343-8228). Wheels is open from 10 to 7 Memorial Day through Labor Day and weekends in the fall. Blades will set you back $5 an hour or $12 for four hours, but that includes all the safety gear: helmets, knee pads, ankle pads and wrist braces.

Try to schedule your first few jaunts for weekdays or a less-than-perfect Saturday or Sunday; the Greenbelt can get dangerously crowded on nice weekends. For an eight-mile round trip, cross the footbridge to *Ann Morrison Park* and head east under Capitol Boulevard to the *BSU* campus. Cross the footbridge into *Julia Davis Park*, then on to *Municipal Park* and back. Don't forget water and snacks, and watch out for cracks and potholes.

For a less-crowded ride, drive your skates to *Municipal* and head east toward *Discovery State Park*. The round trip is a grueling 18 miles, but you can turn around at *Barber Park* or anytime your legs tell you to. The pavement is generally smooth, but watch for gravel near the dirt roads that intersect the path. And be advised that there's often a tailwind going east: the "downhill" ride back may actually be tougher!

Sporting goods stores often have free lessons for beginners and group skates to improve your style and broaden your horizons. The *Sports Exchange* (385-0440) has lessons Saturday mornings and evening skates Tuesdays and Thursdays. *McU's* (342-7734) has a *Downtown Skate Around* at 6:30 Thursday evenings during the summer.

✧ ✧ ✧

Saddle Up!

Bogus Creek Outfitters
Main Street
Kuna
922-4158

Boise Basin Trail Rides
Idaho 21
Idaho City
378-4386

For a state as horse-y as Idaho, there are surprisingly few places you can just ride. You can take lessons or board your own horse (check the phone book), and at least one place (The *Idaho English Riding Company*) lets trained riders go out alone. But in general, if you want a leisurely jog you're going to have to drive a bit first.

The closest stable that runs trail rides is **Bogus Creek Outfitters**, a half-hour away in the Boise Front. They offer western-style rides starting from the First Aid Station at Bogus Basin from about May to October. All rides are led by licensed guides; they range from an hour ($18) to a half-day and are preceded by a short riding lesson. Weekend breakfast rides are $39; evening dinner rides with entertainment go for $49, with non-riders traveling by wagon. A 50% deposit is non-refundable but you can reschedule with 24 hours' notice.

Boise Basin Trail Rides, at the 43-mile marker on Idaho 21, offers trail rides from Memorial Day through Labor Day. Owner Gary Towle and another licensed guide lead groups of up to six people on rides of one hour to two days, over mostly mountainous terrain. A one-hour ride costs about $15, a half-day $45; overnight treks range from $70 to $130 depending on how far you go and what meals you get. Each ride is preceded by a short horsemanship lesson. Children 6 and over are welcome; they can double up with a parent if you want. There's a special 15-minute ride for little kids in which they're mostly led around the driveway or farther afield, depending on their confidence level. Towle will probably start offering horse camps in the summer of 1996.

Reservations are needed Tuesday through Thursday, but the rest of the week you can just drop in. The stable is located on your right four miles north of Idaho City, 1.7 miles past the turnoff to Atlanta.

✧ ✧ ✧

Sports and Recreation

Climb a Rock

The Pinnacle	REI	Outdoor Adventure Pgm.
1875 Century Way	8300 Emerald	Boise State University
376-3641	322-1141	385-1374

Why did Sir Edmund Hillary climb Mt. Everest? Because it was *there*, of course. *Build it and they will climb.*

And build it they did! If you don't know your belayer from your chimney, you're in for a real adventure. With 5,000 square feet of lead, bouldering and traverse areas, **The Pinnacle** at *Wings Center* is Idaho's largest indoor climbing gym. Climbing, the folks at Wings say, builds confidence, coordination and strength.

The Pinnacle teaches climbing (and requires a lesson if you can't pass a skills-and-safety check) but its walls are open for general use Monday through Friday 4 to 9, Saturday 10 to 9 and Sunday noon to 6. Unlimited time costs $10 with shoes and harness, $6 without. Thursday evening is the best time for kids: for $15, with pre-registration, they get two hours of equipment, lessons and games. There are teen beginner lessons Saturday mornings, two-for-one Fridays, $2 off for groups of eight or more, and member discounts. Unless you're coming for a lesson or Thursday "kid time," you must bring your own "belayer" -- that's the person who balances your weight if you fall, so be nice to them!

BSU's Climbing Gym is open to the public Tuesday through Friday and Sunday evenings from 6:30 to 10. *Children under 18 must have a parent with them.* It costs $4 per person plus $3 for equipment.

At **REI** (Recreational Equipment Inc.) you can climb *for free* on Tuesday nights, albeit on less extensive terrain. The wall is open from 6:30 to 8:30, they provide equipment, and they belay (hold the rope) for everyone. Kids over toddler age are welcome, and they'll arrange climbing on Monday or Thursday nights for groups of ten or more.

✪ ❄ ✪

Dribble, Dribble

Fort Boise Community Center
700 Robbins Road
384-4486 or 384-4240

Boise Family YMCA
1050 W. State
344-5501

If you've ever been the parent of a bored teenager, you know what ennui means. Instead of longing for those bygone days when *anything* amused them, send them out to play!

For *just $1 a day*, teens can use **Fort Boise's** game room, gyms and weight room. There's no registration and the fee includes access to showers and locker rooms. It's waived with PAYADA (an anti-drug program) cards, and adults can play for $2. There's drop-in volleyball and basketball on Saturdays during the school year and weekdays in summer; the game and weight rooms are open weekdays until 7 and on weekends. All facilities are open until 11 on Friday nights.

Younger kids can play in neighborhood school open gyms from November through March. It's supervised and less structured than the drop-in games, and free for kids K-12. *Vacation Station* at Fort Boise offers supervised holiday play for kids in grades 3 through high school.

The city's *Parks and Recreation Department*, which operates Fort Boise, offers dozens of classes in art, dance, drama, karate, swimming and tennis for children and youth, as well as camps, clinics and organized sports teams. Call for information on costs and schedule, and be sure to get on the mailing list for the department's *Activity Guide*.

Most of us think of the **YMCA** as a membership organization, and it is, but most of the Y's programs are open to non-members at slightly higher fees. Day passes for kids age 7 through high school are $3; for the same fare, kids 13-18 can attend Saturday evening "Teen Nights." Boise's two Y's specialize in youth sports, with a full complement of lessons, camps, clinics and teams. There are vacation day camps, a preschool program, regular and drop-in day care centers, an after-school program with pick-up from area schools and a New Year's Eve overnighter. And if *you* could stand to get in shape, you can do that too!

✧ ❄ ✧

Sports and Recreation

Take Me Out to the Ball Game . . .

Boise Hawks
Memorial Stadium
5600 Glenwood
322-5020

This is baseball as it used to be: soft summer nights, real grass, hot dogs, popcorn, the 7th inning stretch. All that and a game too!

The **Hawks** came to Boise in 1987 and built Memorial Stadium in 1989. They play short-season minor league ball: 76 games beginning in mid-June and wrapping up in September. Most of the players are chosen in the annual amateur draft in June, many for their first year of professional ball. The Hawks have had an operating agreement with the California Angels since 1990 and have been very successful, winning the Northwest League championship four out of the last five years.

Memorial Stadium holds 4,200 and attendance averages about 3,800 (counting absentee season ticket holders). Apart from the Hawks' success and Boise's general sports-mania, the atmosphere is a big draw. It's a classic small stadium in a gorgeous location; most seats offer spectacular views of the Boise Front. A bit too big to feel "hometown," this is still baseball the way it should be: up close and personal. (So "up close," in fact, that foul balls are a hazard; on the other hand, if you catch one you can easily get it autographed.)

Most seats behind home plate and on the third base side are held by season ticket holders. You can buy reserved bench seats, with backrests, on the first base line, or general admission to the bleachers along right field. The further out you go the more likely you'll be blinded by the sun, but you'll also find more kids and fewer fans who've had too many. There's also a grassy area behind the bleachers where kids can run around, and tables for parents to sit. Sometimes there are activities here: a kid's pitching contest, or maybe a "bouncy castle."

Concession stands serve hot dogs, pizza, beer, nachos and ice cream, and vendors come through almost more often than you'd like. The *Hawk's Nest* opens for full meals at 5:30. Games begin at 7.

✧ ✧ ✧

Ski It!

Bogus Basin Ski Resort
332-5100
342-2100 (snow report)

Boise shares with Albuquerque the rare distinction of having an urban ski resort just minutes away. That prompted me to decide Kate should learn to ski; to keep an eye on her, I needed to learn too. And thus it was that a 4-year-old and her middle-aging Mom found themselves on skis for the first time. Three years later, I'm no closer to being a hotshot, but both of us are still having fun.

As an urban ski area (rather than a destination resort) **Bogus Basin** tends to have older equipment and fewer amenities. But a major expansion is in progress and besides -- lower prices, shorter lift lines and night skiing *more* than make up for any deficiencies.

The area's name came from a couple of 1860's miners who peddled pyrite ("bogus" gold) from Shafer Butte. Bogus operates seven days a week, 10 to 10 on weekdays and 9 to 10 on weekends, from about Thanksgiving through March. Its 2,600 acres sport 45 runs, six chair lifts and an 1800' vertical drop. There are two day lodges, restaurants, a rental shop, day care center, ski school and condos.

In skiing circles Bogus is known as a "well-rounded" mountain: a couple of good beginner runs, excellent intermediate territory and enough expert terrain to satisfy all but the hottest of hotshots. (All are expected to improve with expansion.) There's good snowboarding too. Our biggest complaint is the too-short "bunny hill," served by rope and paddle tows. The snow isn't Utah; it can be icy, but it's still darn good.

After you've had a few lessons and gotten off the bunny hill, put a trail map in your pocket and hop on Morning Star Chair. Exit left, watch out for that first hill, and stay left around the back of Pioneer Lodge. A sharp left puts you on *Pioneer Trail*, a long cat track with a short run at the bottom -- by far the easiest at Bogus. Try *Sunshine*, *Silver Queen* and *Lulu*, then head down the backside on *Buttercup*: it's a long, easy run and one of our favorites, but make sure Bitterroot Chair is running. Try *Smuggler* and *Snoozer* too; if you follow Smuggler all the way to the bottom you'll have to ride to the top of Shafer Butte.

Sports and Recreation

Our favorite long run (just under an hour) starts on Deer Point Chair outside the main Lodge. We make sure Pine Creek is running, then head left across the ridge to *Nugget Cat Track*, *Lower Wildcat Cutoff* and the bottom of Pine Creek Chair. It takes us to the top of Shafer Butte, where we follow *Cabin Traverse* (strong winds sometimes) and *Alpine* back to the bottom. The skiing is perfect for us, but the truth is I do it more for the spectacular views and the peace and quiet.

Skiing *is* expensive but there are ways to cut costs. Rent equipment at first, through *Bogus Basin*, a sporting good store, or *BSU's Outdoor Activities Program*. Then look for clothes and equipment at re-sale stores or the annual November *Ski Swap* at the Fairgrounds. (You can resell the kids' stuff as they outgrow it.) Lift tickets run $28 a day for adults and teens, $19 for kids up to 12 ($18/$15 for night-only; $30/ $21 for day and night), but preschoolers get free season passes, half-price Mondays start in January, and there's a $12 Bitterroot pass weekends and holidays. Consider season passes: they're great guilt-reducers because you can stay only as long as you want. Passes cost considerably less if you buy the summer before.

Skiing with kids can be cumbersome We wear leggings and waterproof shoes for the trip up, and park in the unloading area outside the lodge. I leave our skis in a rack, haul everything else inside and *then* go park the car. There are lockers on the lower floor, but I rarely use them: I don't take valuables, and it's nice to have things handy. Once ensconced at a table, we have a snack and a drink *before* we don boots and bibs. When we're not skiing, I stow skis and poles in a rack or use the employee-attended storage outside (free for season pass holders; $1 a day for others). In addition to the obvious stuff, we take lotion, lip balm, sunblock, water, snacks and an activity book for rest times.

Bogus also offers miles of great *cross-country skiing*, including lessons and rentals. Farther afield, the airport at *Idaho City* is a great place for kids, and there are lots of beginner and intermediate trails in that area. If there's good snow in the valley, you can cross-country right in town: on the *Greenbelt*, in city parks or on golf courses.

For something really different after a day at Bogus check into a *sleigh ride* (p. 116) complete with gourmet dinner!

❄ ❄ ❄

Crack the Whip!

Ice Skating
Idaho City
392-6000 (Skip)
392-4132 (Jim)

Sometime, somewhere, somehow, Boise will have an ice skating rink -- followed in rapid succession, no doubt, by lessons and a hockey team. Meanwhile, if you want to relive childhood memories of crack-the-whip and scraped knees, head for **Idaho City**.

The "rink" at Idaho City is actually a flooded tennis court, and it's a bit of a sometime thing depending on the weather. As soon as the mercury hits freezing, volunteers from the Chamber of Commerce flood it: in a cold winter that could mean skating from early December through March; in a really warm winter, there might be no skating at all.

When Mother Nature cooperates, volunteers open the rink between 9 and 10 every day and keep it open as long as there's enough light to see. There's usually an old heater around to warm your frosty hands, and skates (in children's and adult sizes) are available for rent.

This isn't Rockefeller Center, so bundle up and bring plenty of hot chocolate. You can combine this adventure with *cross-country skiing* (p. 73) or a *sleigh ride* (p. 116), then warm those old bones with a steamy dip at *Warm Springs Resort* (p. 128).

❄ ❄ ❄

Joy Ride

Camel's Back Park	Idaho 21	Bogus Basin Road
13th & Heron	N. of Lucky Peak	S. of Bogus Basin

Where I grew up we called it coasting. Others call it sledding, or even sleigh-riding, but whatever you call it, it's a kid's thrill and a parent's headache. (One of my fondest memories of childhood is tobogganing with friends on a deserted country road in the moonlight; no doubt my mother's memory of that same evening is a bit different!)

Because sledding is not without risks, the first issue is the child's age. My daughter tried it at 2 with a parent and at 4 by herself, and was lucky enough to sustain no permanent damage. If I had it to do over, though, I might wait a bit longer, since head injuries are nothing to fool with. They're less common on a sled than a bike, but helmets still make sense. They're not de rigueur yet, but it's probably just a matter of time.

The second issue is the sled itself. My bottom line is one that steers: our mainstay is a classic runner-type, but we also found a plastic job that steers a bit and has a pretty decent brake to boot. I reject those little plastic disks; they're easy to pull up but uncontrollable going down.

Boise needs a couple of groomed hills, age-appropriate and far from traffic. The closest thing is **Camel's Back Park**, at 13th and Heron in the North End. The slopes range from itty-bitty to terrifying, but it's *very* popular and can get dangerously crowded. Moreover, unless it's a good snow the traffic wears it down to dirt pretty quickly.

Out of town a bit, but convenient to east Boise, there's a good hill just off **Idaho 21** on the left, 3.1 miles north of the turnoff for Sandy Point. (If you get to the Hilltop Cafe you've missed it.) There's plenty of parking on the right, but be careful crossing the busy highway. When there's no snow in the valley, or you're going skiing, try any of several pull-outs along **Bogus Basin Road** south of the ski resort.

❄ ❄ ❄

Fairs and Festivals

Fairs and Festivals

Introduction

From New Year's Eve 'til Christmas, the Treasure Valley overflows with festivals of every color and stripe. We celebrate *everything* here, from historic preservation and old-time fiddlin' to the Oregon Trail pioneers and the Boise River. And since this is a family town, almost every celebration is designed with kids in mind.

As you'd expect, fairs and festivals concentrate themselves in the summer months (you can, if you want, celebrate something different almost every day for the entire month of June). But we find something to cheer about the rest of the year as well: New Year's Eve downtown, Halloween at a haunted house, Christmas on an old-time trolley.

The big four -- the *Boise River Festival*, the *Western Idaho Fair*, *Art in the Park* and the *Festival of Trees* -- are publicized within an inch of their lives. They're here too, of course, but so are a lot of lesser-known events: free art lessons in the park, a chance to try your hand at blacksmithing and do laundry on a washboard, unique celebrations of Boise's Greek and Jewish communities, and a wonderful re-enactment of Oregon Trail pioneers crossing the Snake River.

Though big-sister Boise dominates the festival scene, the area's smaller communities more than pull their weight. In these pages you'll find guides to down home celebrations in Meridian, Eagle, Emmett, Weiser and Idaho City, and a list of county fairs and rodeos.

Packing for fair-going is simple: think of everything you might need and then take more. Seriously, it's always better to over-pack than under-pack, especially when you're going someplace you haven't been before. Chairs, extra sweaters and water bottles are part of my car's standard equipment, along with whatever my daughter's current critical needs are. Most of the time everything stays put, but when kids need something they *really* need it, so why not have it? Maybe then you'll never find yourselves, as we did, miles from anywhere, with no diapers!

Food abounds at all these celebrations, of course, albeit for a price. It isn't usually the most nutritious food either, so be kind to your wallet *and* your body having a healthy snack before you go. Insist on bathroom visits too; many of these celebrations have only portables.

First Night

Downtown
New Year's Eve
343-6567

Can't get a babysitter? Tired of the booze and the hassles? Want to ring in the new year with those you love most? This year, celebrate New Year's Eve *with* your kids, in downtown Boise.

First Night started in Boston and has spread to 135 cities around the country. Boise's version, which will debut the last night of 1995, is alcohol-free and jam-packed with talent. The family-centered celebration is sponsored by IJA Productions, a non-profit arts presenter.

Since kids always have more energy than adults it makes sense that they start partying earlier, at an afternoon smorgasbord of hands-on arts workshops. (Mask-making is a surefire hit.) At 5:30 they take projects in hand, grab parents, friends and neighbors and march Mardi-Gras style through the streets of downtown. The evening's centerpiece -- dubbed *Arts by Starlight* -- gets underway at 7. In a series of indoor and outdoor venues ranged along 8th Street south of the Grove, party-goers partake of theater, dance, painting, sculpture, poetry, and music of all stripes, from opera to rock 'n' roll. The 30 to 40-minute performances continue 'til 11 and are repeated throughout the evening; their length and content are geared to appeal to children as well as adults. The countdown to midnight begins at 11, with fireworks and a community chorus (singing *Auld Lang Syne*, we presume).

As if sharing the new year with your kids weren't a big enough draw in itself, consider the relative cost. What would you spend on an evening out: dinner, drinks, babysitter? At least $50, right, and more like $100? Until December 15, you can buy admission buttons for *all* the First Night events for *just $5 apiece*; after that they cost $7. And kids under 6 get in *free*. You really can't *afford* to pass this up!

Pat that Drum, Hold that Horn!

Boise Philharmonic Family Concert
Morrison Center
January
344-7849

You've heard of a Petting Zoo; now meet a *Petting Orchestra*, where kids can pat a drum, hold a horn and stroke a violin bow. The instruments aren't as cuddly, but the sound is music to a parent's ear.

The Boise Philharmonic's annual **Family Concert** is the perfect place to introduce your children to serious music. Held on a Sunday afternoon in January, the 50-minute concert offers "real" music selected and shortened to match the average preschooler's attention span. The personable conductor carries on a running monologue with his young audience, and best of all, dress is casual and wiggling *is* permitted.

Good as the concert is, it's the *pre*-concert festivities that have drawn more and more families since this event's inception. Besides playing real instruments (cleaned between each use), kids can practice conducting, compose music on a computer, color in a musical theme, and unearth pieces of instruments in a vat of dried beans.

Still in its infancy, the Family Concert sold out in its third year. Tickets are available through *Select-A-Seat* (see p. 28); they cost $3 for kids and students and $6 for adults. For information about the Philharmonic's kid-friendly *dress rehearsals*, see p. 31.

Scrambled Eggs

Easter Egg Scramble
Ann Morrison Park
Early Spring

Try to imagine 400 kids pushing and shoving, baskets in hand, greed in their eyes, determined to get that last plastic egg before the next kid does. If you have trouble seeing it, you haven't been to the **Easter Egg Scramble** lately.

Greed? Shoving? Plastic eggs? Doesn't sound much like the spirit of Easter, does it? Well, it isn't. And if you want my opinion, kids over 5 shouldn't go -- just like kids over 12 shouldn't go trick-or-treating (and *no one* should if they won't wear a costume). But for the little ones, who are often too timid to even scoop up the eggs, let alone push and shove, this annual scramble-in-the-park is worth doing at least once.

The date varies from year to year, but it's traditionally held the Saturday of the weekend before Easter. Kids are (thankfully) sorted by age and the little ones go first, so you don't have to wait or stay too long. And what's in those eggs everyone's so excited about? Why, what else? Candy, little toys, coupons, stuff like that. *Now* you understand!

If the philosophy behind this kind of thing offends you, or if you want to augment it with something a bit more traditional, check the paper for real Easter egg hunts or organize your own. Happy Hunting!

Fairs and Festivals

The Sounds of Music

Boise Music Week
Early May

This is one tradition that's grown better with age. For ten days in and around the first week in May, Boise comes alive with the sounds of music: every kind of music, and the best part is, it's all free!

Music Week started in 1919, when a returning soldier realized that Boise was too far off the beaten path to attract traveling shows. The all-volunteer effort hasn't missed a year since then.

The week kicks off with *School Night*, a fast-paced evening of vocal and instrumental performances by groups from schools around the valley. No tickets are needed for this Friday event at the Boise State University Pavilion. Saturday afternoon brings *Music in the Park*, a four-hour showcase of local groups at the bandshell in Julia Davis Park.

No tickets are needed for *Church Night* either, an inter-denominational celebration of religious music by groups from churches around the valley, or for the weekday-noon *organ concerts*, held Monday through Thursday at St. Michael's Episcopal Church and on Friday, compete with film and sing-along, at the Egyptian Theater.

You *will* need free tickets for the *Showcase* of musical talent offered Monday and Tuesday evening at Boise High School auditorium, and for Music Week's *piece de resistance*: its annual Broadway musical. This all-local, all-volunteer production offers six performances at the Morrison Center, Wednesday through Saturday evenings at 8 and Friday and Saturday afternoons at 2. Most shows will appeal at least to older children and all performances are open to them, although the Friday afternoon matinee is geared toward seniors and the hearing-impaired.

It's all free, but that doesn't mean you can get in: the musical *always* plays to full houses and Showcase is getting there; watch for the coupon in the newspaper about two weeks ahead and send it in *pronto*.

Orchids and Onions

Historic Preservation Week
334-3861
May

Each year, the Idaho Historic Preservation Council awards "orchids and onions" to the best and worst examples of historic preservation. More to the point for parents, **Historic Preservation Week** also offers walking tours and a silent movie appropriate for older children, and a "history fair" guaranteed to appeal to the child in all of us.

The walks change each year, often taking strollers along Harrison Boulevard or Warm Springs Avenue, around the North End or through historic downtown buildings. For most children, though, the highlights will be the history fair at *Bown House* (see p. 83) and a silent film show complete with pipe organ at the historic *Egyptian Theater*.

Originally called the Ada, the theater stands at the corner of Main and Capitol and is, by all accounts, the best example of Egyptian revival architecture in the Northwest. (The revival of that style was sparked by the discovery of King Tut's tomb in 1922.) It cost $160,000 in 1927 and though threatened by redevelopment on more than one occasion, continues to offer first-run and revival movies. Even children too young to appreciate the history will be charmed by the colorful decor and old-fashioned feel, so far removed from the antiseptic theaters of today. There's even a full-fledged balcony -- the kind you and I remember!

Far removed, too, are the films themselves: black-and-white, silent, often filled with sight gags and slapstick, accompanied by sound effects on the theater's historic pipe organ. Though children probably won't give up their diet of Babysitters and Turtles in favor of this, at least they'll get a better perspective on the cinematic ancestry of their heroes.

Fairs and Festivals

A Walk through the Past . . .

Bown House
2020 E. Victory Rd.
338-3400
May

Once a year this restored 1879 house is the site of a "history fair," where kids try their hands at a variety of 19th century crafts and chores. Like the *Discovery Center* (p. 6) and *Arts for Kids* (p. 85), this is learning at its best: no lectures, just down-and-dirty hands-on doing.

Held on a Saturday afternoon in May as a kickoff to *Historic Preservation Week*, the fair offers tours of the **Bown House**, including its school room, kitchen and parlor. But the real action is outside, where kids stamp leather, make candles, churn butter, rope a plastic "calf," spin wool, make corn husk dolls, and wash and iron the old-fashioned way.

There's period entertainment too: history plays, frontier storytelling, banjos, clog dancing, knife throwing, muzzle loading, cow-chip carving and even a "con man," complete with card tricks, magic, miracle cures and get-rich-quick schemes!

Admission is free. Bown House is located on the grounds of *Riverside Elementary School*, at the southeast end of Park Center Boulevard. The two-story sandstone structure is one of the oldest homes in the Boise Valley. Built by pioneer ranchers Joseph and Temperance Bown, is was considered the finest dwelling outside of the downtown area, and is listed on the National Register of Historic Places. It served as a school, social center and prominent landmark on the Oregon Trail, and is now owned by the Boise School District and used for their 4th grade Heritage Education program. Restoration is through a joint stewardship program with the Idaho Historic Preservation Council.

See p. 45 for a description of another fascinating *history fair*. For other events during *Historic Preservation Week*, see p. 82.

It's Greek to Me

Greek Food Festival
Ste. Constantine & Helen Greek Orthodox Church
27th and Bannock
June

Boise's small Greek community celebrates summer with an outdoor food and dance festival that grows more popular -- and more crowded -- each year. If you really *hate* long lines, come for lunch. But be advised that evenings are a lot more fun: the air is balmy, the crowd festive and the atmosphere more exotic.

Spanning the first weekend in June, from 11 to 9 Friday and 11 to 9 Saturday, the **Greek Food Festival** offers a reassuringly predictable menu: souvlaki (skewered pork), gyros (meat in a pita), spanikopita (spinach pie), dolmathes (stuffed grape leaves), stefatho (beef & onions in tomato sauce) and pastitsio (Greek lasagna) are the staples, supplemented by savory rice pilafi, fasolia yahni (green beans in a tangy tomato sauce), rolls, salad and great desserts, plus soft drinks, beer, wine and coffee. Everything is tasty, though some items may be a bit too spicy for children. Admission is $1 by donation, free for kids under 12; a family of four will spend about $25 for dinner and dessert.

Adults may come for the food, but it's the atmosphere that fascinates children. The hypnotic music, exuberant dancing and snatches of overheard Greek seem to mesmerize them, and add a welcome multicultural note to a largely homogenous community.

The music, sadly, is recorded; the dancing, however, is anything but. On a warm Saturday night you'll swear every Greek in Boise, from smallest child to senior citizen, is in on it! When the "official" dancers aren't performing anyone can get into the act, and non-Greek children often do. Just be sure to take a break to tour the lovely church.

While I admit to occasional crowd-induced frustration, this is still a family favorite; all it needs is a tuneup. With more space available now, there ought to be a way to shorten up the food lines.

I'm Not Messy -- I'm Creative!

Arts for Kids
Julia Davis Park
336-4936
June

In a month jam-packed with festivals, this one stands out: free arts and crafts lessons in the park, courtesy of the Boise City Arts Commission and the Parks and Recreation Department.

Arts for Kids appeals primarily on the elementary set. Held on a Saturday in Julia Davis Park, it offers upwards of 30 different workshops from clay sculpture, weaving and watercolor to music, dance and origami. Most are open to kids 6 and up, but a few -- like calligraphy and etching -- have a higher age limit. Many of the workshops produce projects the kids can take home.

Each child can register for up to three workshops in either the morning or afternoon session. There are also a few activities for preschoolers that don't require registration (but do require parents to stay with their children), and a lunchtime performance of music, dance and drama for the whole family, suitable for picnicking. Registration is by mail only, beginning in May, and the most popular workshops fill up fast. Call for an application, but if you miss the deadline go anyway: spots are sometimes available on a first-come, first-served basis.

While you're in the park, consider a ride on the *Tour Train* (p. 43) or a visit to the *Boise Art Museum* (p. 30), the *Idaho State Historical Museum* (p. 45), the *Discovery Center* (p. 6) or *Zoo Boise* (p. 10).

Pottery, Painting and the Past

Arts & Crafts Festival
Idaho City
392-4553
June

Idaho City is *different*. Part hard-living mountain town, part winter sports haven, part artsy-craftsy hippie, it both lives up to and defies its past as a gold mining boom town -- the Pacific Northwest's largest city in the late 1860's.

Held on the second weekend in June, the annual **Idaho City Arts & Crafts Festival** leans a little -- not too much -- toward the hippie. Open from about 10 a.m. to 8 p.m. on Saturday and 10 to 5 on Sunday, the fair offers some 80 artists and artisans, a dozen or so food booths, live entertainment, Smokey the Bear and a crafts area for kids. It also provides the perfect opportunity to explore this fascinating town.

When you've had your fill of the fair, head for the *Boise Basin Museum* on Montgomery Street one block west of Main. The museum building was once a bookstore and a post office. Check out the old *fire station* at 511 Montgomery and the *Masonic Hall* near Montgomery and Wall, then drive down Main Street to see the town's original *schoolhouse*, the *Miner's Exchange*, the *Boise Basin Mercantile* and the headquarters for the *Idaho World* newspaper. Poke around the shops a bit to get a feel for the unique ambiance of the town.

In its heyday, Idaho City was home to 6,200 people -- 5,600 of them men. It boasted three dozen saloons, two dozen law offices, two bowling alleys, a mattress factory, a photographer's studio and a hospital. It also burned four times.

Idaho City is an hour and northeast of Boise: 20 winding miles via Warm Springs Avenue and Idaho 21. As you approach the town you'll see the sad remains of years of placer (stream) mining in the piles of rock on either side of the road. About a mile south of town you'll pass *Warm Springs Plunge*, a pleasant place for a dip in geothermally-heated water (p. 128). *Boise Basin Trail Rides* (p. 68) is four miles north.

Fairs and Festivals

Get Soaked!

Eagle Fun Days
June

This old-time small town celebration just might leave you dripping. In truth, though, it's more likely the kids who'll get wet, since the volunteer firefighters in the parade *try* to spray only willing victims.

Eagle Fun Days includes a breakfast, a cookoff, draft horses, games, food booths and what's billed as the "World's Largest Rocky Mountain Oyster Feed." (Rocky Mountain oysters are bull's testicles, but try explaining *that* to your 6-year-old!) Just head out State Street; you can't miss it, and you'll have some good old-fashioned fun.

⚑ ⚑ ⚑

So That's Where Milk Comes From

Meridian Dairy Days
888-2817
June

As rapidly as the cow population of Meridian is declining, Idaho's fastest-growing community *needs* this reminder of its past. No longer strictly an agricultural show, **Dairy Days** now includes all the events we've come to expect from "festivals" along with its down-on-the-farm roots. For confirmed people-watchers, there's the added bonus of eavesdropping as new suburbanites mingle with longtime farm families.

Dairy Days is held the third weekend in June, Wednesday through Sunday, in the city park at the corner of East Third and Franklin and the Dairy Barn next door. It kicks off with the annual Dairy Princess banquet, followed by a pancake feed Thursday night, parade Friday night and auction Saturday afternoon. There's a carnival, food booths, a petting zoo and a full range of 4-H and FFA fitting and showing events. There are bathrooms in the park and barn, Porta-Potties elsewhere.

⚑ ⚑ ⚑

Wild Rides and Cherry Pies

Emmett Cherry Festival
City Park
365-3485
June

For us, this fair is just the right size: bigger than the annual fetes in *Meridian* and *Eagle* (p. 87), smaller than the *Western Idaho Fair* (p. 96). In early June, the weather's usually just right too.

The **Cherry Festival** traditionally starts with a *team roping competition* at the Fairgrounds Sunday and Monday of the first full week in June. Monday's also the *Miss Gem County Pageant* at the Middle School; by Wednesday or Thursday, the fair's in full swing at City Park.

Aside from the usual rides and games, this fair has some unique touches: *classic cars*, a *beer garden*, *Art in the Park* and a truly impressive *quilt show* at the Middle School. But it's the community itself that makes the Cherry Festival a classic: thanks to local people, it has one of the best parades around, food just different enough to offer an occasional surprise, true small-town entertainment and even a few games still run by local clubs. What we'd like to see more of, strangely enough, is *cherries*. I know production is going down and sometimes the weather doesn't cooperate, but in good years at least, the sweet fruit should lend a larger signature touch to this already-excellent event.

Take State Street (Highway 44) west through Eagle and turn right on Highway 16 to Emmett. Make a right at the intersection and follow signs to the park. Allow the best part of a day for a visit, and remember that bathrooms are mostly Porta-Potties and grass is tough on strollers.

If you like this one, watch for other Emmett events, including *Harvest Fest* in the fall and *Cruise Night* in mid-summer. For a delightful *pick-your-own-fruit* adventure, see p. 119.

Fairs and Festivals

Deli Days

Congregation Ahavath Beth Israel
11th and State
June

A smaller affair than the *Greek Festival* (p. 84), this lunch-or-dinner outing nonetheless offers a fascinating glimpse of Boise's active Jewish community, as well as a look at a lovely and historic building.

Jews have lived in Idaho for more than 100 years, and the Gem State holds the distinction of having elected the first Jewish governor in the nation: Moses Alexander, who served from 1915 to 1919.

Held on a Thursday and Friday in June -- usually the second or third weekend -- **Deli Days** serves up bagels, lox, sandwiches, salads and desserts from 11 to 7 each day. The food is reasonably priced, served cafeteria style and eaten under pleasant canopies on the side lawn. Cookbooks and T-shirts are for sale, but the main attraction is the chance to tour one of the oldest and most attractive synagogues west of the Mississippi and learn a bit about Jewish theology and culture. Space is at a premium here and lunchtime can get crowded, so you may want to "snack" the kids and hold out for a late lunch or early dinner.

⚑ ⚑ ⚑

Take Me Out With the Crowd . . .

Boise River Festival
205 N. 10th St.
383-7318
Late June

What can I say? Boise's premiere event, spanning four days in late June, is hot, crowded and often frustrating. But it's also friendly, exciting and infinitely varied. You owe it to yourself to go at least once.

The **River Festival's** signature event is a *lighted float parade*, held Friday and Saturday night starting about 10. No longer on the river, the floats are just as delightful on the street and a lot easier to see. Scout a spot in advance, get there early, have someone guard your chairs and explore downtown Boise in full evening celebration. Check out the *carnival* on Front Street and *Bite of Boise* in the Grove. Keep close track of the kids: the Grove, especially, will be wall-to-wall people. For a different kind of parade, less thrilling for adults but equally so for small children, don't miss the Saturday morning *River Giants*.

Hot air balloons play a big part in this fest, but they'll require you to get up early or stay up late. Pick a Thursday, Friday or Saturday morning, drag the kids out of bed at 6 and start scanning the skies: on a clear morning, the sight of a dozen balloons drifting across the sky is enchanting. For a close-up view head for Ann Morrison Park: if you time it right, you can see the balloons on the ground -- some in the shape of hot dogs, cartoon characters, even a castle -- then watch them rise into the air. Parking isn't bad that early and crowds are minimal, but the noise and flames may frighten small children. If they pass that test, head back to the park one evening for *Nite Glow*. The balloons don't fly but they do rise on cables and against the night sky it's a sight to behold.

Appropriately, the festival ends with a literal bang: the best *fireworks* I've seen anywhere since Idaho's Centennial celebration. Of course there's a lot more going on in Ann Morrison Park as well, including some of the best entertainment of the entire festival, so come early, stake out your spot and wander around. Just be sure you're back at your chairs early; for safety reasons, much of the park is cordoned off starting well before the fireworks themselves. Choosing a spot can be tricky: you want a clear view of the southeast side of the park, that will

Fairs and Festivals

enable you to leave without crossing the footbridge on the Greenbelt: it always turns into an awful bottleneck. The last two years, our choice has been the east end of the park, south of the picnic pavilion. The view is great, and we've gotten home faster than we did in earlier years.

Those are the biggies, then: the Nite-Lite Parade, River Giants Parade, Nite Glow, the carnival, Bite of Boise and the fireworks. But don't neglect the "little" events either: they're what bring us back year after year in search of new adventures. Among our favorite "discoveries" have been the spectacular *sand sculpture* built as you watch in Julia Davis Park; the equally-spectacular *castle* made from donated canned goods; the delightful, sappy *Kids and Pets on Parade*; the *storytellers*, both professional adult and charming child; the Mayor's annual *Soap Box Derby*; and the yearly adventures of *Justin Time* and *Captain Air*, a mostly-wonderful musical play for children (one year it was *awful*!)

Other activities for kids include *Elsie the Cow* and her *train ride* around Ann Morrison Park, *boat races* and a *miniature golf tournament* at the Fun Spot, a kid's *fishing clinic*, children's *fun run*, the wild, silly but somehow funny *Great Breakfast Scramble*, the *Children's Talent Show*, *Smokey the Bear*, a *maze* made from office partitions, and the usual assortment of clowns, crafts, games and face-painting.

⚑ ⚑ ⚑

Fiddlin' Around

National Oldtime Fiddlers' Contest
Weiser High School Gymnasium
1-800-437-1280
June

It's not for nothing that Weiser calls itself the "Fiddling Capital of the World." Spanning six days in late June, the **National Oldtime Fiddlers' Contest** is the biggie of the year, drawing some 300 musicians from around the country in categories from *Small Fry* to *Senior-Senior*.

The competition runs from early morning 'til late at night, culminating in the *National Grand Championship* on Saturday night. Tickets go from $2 for a day pass to $15 for a Saturday reserved seat, and you simply *must* take the kids to at least one session. The *Junior* (14-18) or *Junior-Junior* (5-13) are both good choices, and though the *Small Fry's* music may not be up to much, there's nothing like the sight of a little 3-year-old rosinin' up her bow and fiddlin' her little heart out.

The music doesn't stop at the gym door either. There's an early morning jam session and dance at the *Senior Center*, daily workshops, and Native American music and dance at the *Intermountain Cultural Center*. But some of the best music can be heard in parking lots and campgrounds, as fiddlers engage in impromptu jam sessions. Even if you don't go to a formal session, this music is well worth the trip.

The National is now a full-blown festival, complete with carnival, pony rides, petting zoo, quilt and craft exhibits, and a Saturday-night parade, barbecue and street dance. Tickets for sessions can be ordered by phone or mail or purchased the day of the event at the high school.

Weiser is 70 miles from Boise, so a long day will get you there and back with plenty of time to attend a session and poke around. If you want to stay, grab a room or a campsite early; everything in this small town fills up fast. Expect a lot of music and not much sleep! Take I-84 west to the Fruitland-Payette Exit and go about 20 miles north on 95.

Fairs and Festivals

Fireworks on Parade

Parade and Fireworks
362-5780
Fourth of July

Here's a Cinderella story for you: four years ago, Boise's **Independence Day parade** was DOA, its organizers deciding to put all their energies into the *Holiday Parade* (p. 102). Enter Karen Valinske and her white knight, Chevron Pipeline. She ran it that year; the next year, her father, Peter, took over; the year after that, her mother, Lavada. Now the Valinskes are looking for someone to take over from *them*, but if no new white knight appears, I'm sure they'll soldier on.

The parade starts at 6:30 and runs about two hours along a downtown route. There are some 130 entries, but it'll be over in plenty of time for you to get to the fireworks.

Boise's **4th of July fireworks** have been overshadowed by the upstart *River Festival* (p. 90), but instead of folding their tent organizers have fought back with upgrades. So show some gratitude: pack your blankets, chairs and binoculars, fill the cooler and stake out a likely spot. Good places are closely guarded secrets, like hot springs and fishing holes, but there are some rules: Go early. Get closer than you think. Get up high or right underneath. And check sightlines in advance. (One memorable year at Memorial Stadium, we had a great view of the trees!)

We like the epicenter, inside the *Western Idaho Fairgrounds*, with the bursts going off right over our heads. Otherwise, your best bet is up the hill on Glenwood. It used to be a prime spot before development made most of the best seats private; early birds can still luck out. Getting home is another matter. No matter how you go you'll get stuck in traffic, so dress the little ones in pajamas and bring plenty of patience!

🏴 🏴 🏴

Ride 'em Cowboy!

Snake River Stampede
Nampa
July

Caldwell Night Rodeo
Caldwell
August

Whether you're an avid rodeo fan or just curious, the historic **Snake River Stampede** is the place to go: large enough for good competition, small enough to still feel friendly.

The 80-year-old rodeo has seen its share of stars: homegrown champs like Dee Pickett and Dean Oliver, celebrities like Gene Autry, Pat Boone, Barbara Mandrell and Reba McEntire. In 1996, the Stampede moves from its longtime home on Garrity Boulevard to a brand new 12-thousand seat facility north of I-84 just west of Robinson Road.

The five-night rodeo kicks off with a Saturday morning parade. There's entertainment at 7:15 each night, with competition beginning at 8 and including such events as bareback and saddle bronc riding, bull riding, calf roping, steer wrestling and barrel racing. In 1995, ticket prices were $5 to $12, half-price for children under 10 on Kid's Night. Buy them at *Karcher Mall* in Nampa, *Select-a-Seat* (p. 28) or at the gate beginning at 6:30 each evening. To avoid the occasional fan who's had too much, ask about special seating in alcohol-free sections.

If you miss the Stampede, try the **Caldwell Night Rodeo** in August. This week-long event kicks off with a Buckaroo Breakfast on Saturday morning and includes team roping Monday evening (free) and entertainment starting at 7:15 each evening (6:30 on Tuesday). Rodeo events start at 8 Tuesday through Saturday, and each evening winds up with a wild horse race. Tickets run $5 to $10, with no reserved seating.

Fairs and Festivals

One More River to Cross . . .

Three Island Crossing
Glenns Ferry
August

This annual history lesson is learning as it should be: dirty, dusty, sweaty, risky, interactive and *fun*. On the second weekend in August, a stalwart group of people and animals re-create the pioneers' crossing of the river the native peoples called Shoshone -- now known as the Snake.

The 50,000 emigrants who reached **Three Island** in the mid-1800's faced a potentially deadly choice: crossing the river might cost them their lives or possessions, but the alternative was dry, rough and treacherous. About half chose to cross; not all of them made it.

The two crossing places at Three Island were attractive for the islands and sandbars that served as stepping stones. Still, it was the toughest river crossing on the way west: the water could reach 8' deep, the current was swift, and people, animals and things were lost.

The annual August re-creation was first performed in 1985. A replica of Gus Glenn's ferry from the 1870's leads the way at 10 a.m. At 11, led by Indian guides in traditional garb, "pioneers" on horseback guide a half-dozen wagons pulled by mules and oxen across the river. There's a parade, music, a breakfast, a barbecue, canoe races, a "shootout," a beard contest and a re-creation of an Indian encampment. Admission to Three Island State Park is $3 for adults and $1 for children.

From Boise take I-84 east to Exit 121 at Glenns Ferry. Follow Main Street through town and across the railroad tracks to the river; signs will take you from there. There's bleacher seating, but it's wiser to bring your own chairs and an umbrella to ward off the hot summer sun.

There are more than 1,700 miles of the Oregon Trail in Idaho, and remnants are visible in many places (see pp. 44). To learn more, read *Oregon Trail in Idaho*, available free at the *Idaho Historical Museum* (p. 45), visit the excellent Interpretive Center in Baker, Oregon, or try your hand at "pioneering" with the CD ROM game *Oregon Trail II*.

It's Ba-a-a-ck . . .

**Western Idaho Fair
Chinden & Glenwood
August**

Face it: unless you turn off the TV and live like hermits for the month of August, you *aren't* going to escape the **Western Idaho Fair**. So be a sport: take the kids and turn it into an excellent adventure.

Let's admit right up front that the fair is hot, expensive, bad for your diet and full of things that serve no earthly purpose but to take your money and upset your stomach. But if you can summon the serenity to accept the things you can't change, the courage to change the things you can and the wisdom to know the difference, you'll be in good shape.

One thing you *can't* change is rides, so don't fight it; limit the damage instead. In 1995, using advance-purchase admissions and coupons for unlimited-ride wristbands, a family of four could get in and give the kids more than enough rides to make them sick for $25. (Another $6 if you need to accompany small children, or just like spinning 80 mph upside-down and backwards.) Wristbands are for afternoon *or* evening; evenings are cooler and prettier, but hordes of teenagers can intimidate small children and make separation a frightening possibility.

I can muster little serenity for the games, which seem to get worse each year. I've even begun to long for the rigged games of my youth: you couldn't win them either, but at least you knew why. Today's games aren't rigged; they're just impossible, or cost more than the prize is worth. Skip the ones that guarantee kids a prize: that kind of "self-esteem" you don't need; look instead for one the child *might* be able to win that doesn't cost *too* much more than the prize is worth.

By contrast, I am perfectly serene about fair food -- which is, by definition, greasy, sugary and delicious. Super parents, I suppose, would spend hours searching out the few nutritious items, but we prefer to indulge and be grateful it only lasts a week. (Seriously, a healthy snack before leaving home is the best antidote to over-indulgence.)

Those, then, are the inevitabilities; on now to the *real* fair. Its essence is, of course, both western and agricultural, and no visit is

Fairs and Festivals

complete without stops at the large animal barns, the surprisingly authentic little mining town and the record-setting vegetables. My "must do" list also includes the llama barn (where you can lead the gentle creatures or watch their babies frolic), the small animal building (with drinking fountain, bathrooms and the coolest air around) and a barn tour. We always try to work in a bit of the horse show as well, some large and small animal judging, and the dog obedience trials. In the exposition buildings we skip the commercial vendors, admire the photography, gape at humongous vegetables and test our ability to tell wheat from oats.

The success of a fair trip lies in the planning. For your wallet's sake you'll probably want to go only once, so get a schedule, sit down with the kids and make your "don't miss" list. Compromise and cross out, then buy your advance admissions and get wristband coupons.

On that day, go early, bring your list, take a stroller (even for kids who rarely use them) and get ID bands for children too young to remember their names. Choose a place to meet if you get separated or choose to split up (the cooling waterfall and pond at the corner of the midway and food row is our choice), adopt a leisurely pace, and enjoy!

Also in August, the **Payette County Fair and Rodeo** (New Plymouth; 278-3150), **Gem County Fair & Rodeo** (Emmett; 365-6828), **Valley County Fair and Rodeo** (Cascade; 634-7430). In July, the **Canyon County Fair** (Caldwell; 454-7498), Elmore County Fair and Rodeo (Glenns Ferry; 366-2725), **Weiser Valley Roundup** (437-1280).

Art in the Park

Julia Davis Park
345-8330
September

This get-a-start-on-Christmas festival the weekend after Labor Day is designed mainly for adults, but kids love it too -- as long as you aren't pushing a stroller and don't run afoul of someone's dog.

Actually, there *are* paved paths you can use with a stroller, but with the number of booths **Art in the Park** has, many are spread out on the grass. If you take a bike chain you can lock your stroller to a tree and continue on foot. The park has bathrooms and a drinking fountain.

There's food a-plenty here (maybe *too* a-plenty; the fair was just last week!) and lot of activities for kids, but the main draw are the hundreds of talented artists and artisans who display their wares in the shade of the park's huge old trees. You'll find photography, watercolors, oil painting, pottery, weaving, furniture, toys and a whole lot more, all in a lovely setting for an afternoon-in-the-park.

Art in the Park opens Friday morning at 10 and closes Sunday at 6. The crowds get thick but people are pretty mellow; just remember to keep an eye on your kids, and set a meeting place in case you get lost.

Fairs and Festivals

A Fair with an Attitude

Hyde Park Street Fair
North End Neighborhood Association
September
344-9783

The North End's annual street fair has always been a little different: moderate-to-liberal politically, heavy on the causes, with a dose of leftover 60's hippiness. If that's your style, or if you just want a relaxed afternoon in a fun neighborhood, give it a try.

Spanning three blocks along 13th Street between Sherman and Brumback and a few side streets along the way, the two-day **Hyde Park Street Fair** is an eclectic mix of artists, peddlers, food booths, political activists and entertainment. It's a friendly place: if you live in the neighborhood you'll meet neighbors; if you don't, you'll make new friends.

Usually held the third weekend in September, the fair puts an enormous strain on already-limited parking in this urban neighborhood. In 1995 organizers responded by sponsoring a *shuttle* from the old K-Mart parking lot (now Micron) at Americana and Riverside. Since things change from year to year, check to see if it's running.

The fair takes place in the heart of Boise's history. *Hyde Park* was developed in the late 1800's, the city's oldest shopping center outside of downtown. Its buildings are a mix of late Queen Anne and early Colonial Revival, and it's currently enjoying a renaissance heavily rooted in food and antiques. Four new businesses have moved in within the last year and at least three more are coming, joining such old-timers as *Lucky 13* (a pizza parlor-cum-cafe recently featured on the cover of *Outdoor* magazine), *Idaho River Sports*, *Pacific Rim* (another restaurant), the *Hyde Park Book Shop*, *Vince's Barber Shop* and *Blue Moon Antiques*. Fair time is a crowded-but-fun time to poke around.

▷ ▷ ▷

Nightmare on 9th Street

Idaho Shakespeare Festival
8th Street Marketplace
October

  Jack-o-lanterns and bunny costumes are fine for little kids, but what those "grown up" 10-year-olds *really* need is a good old-fashioned haunted house. Courtesy of the multi-talented *Idaho Shakespeare Festival* and the *Family Entertainment Group*, Boise has just the thing.

  Each October, the company rents an old warehouse building in the 8th Street Marketplace area, and proceeds to spook it up. Visitors go in groups through the four levels of dark passageways and creaking staircases, meeting ghosts, goblins and ghouls at every turn. No one *yet* has failed to return, but who knows what lies around that corner . . .

  Nightmare on 9th Street is creepy enough to give most kids a thrill, but this haunted house is really more theatrical than terrifying. It relies more on masks and costumes than axes and chain saws, and that ghoulish-looking character is more likely to join your group than to jump out and scream. Still, it's no place for small children or those who are easily frightened or afraid of the dark. Our 7-year-old enjoyed it, but she stuck close to us and probably wouldn't have made it the year before.

  The nightmare begins in mid-October and continues through All Hallow's Eve, weekends at first, then every night. It's open Sunday through Thursday from 7 to 10, Friday and Saturday from 7 to midnight. As you'd expect, lines get longer later in the evening and as Halloween approaches; it may be worth it to teenagers to hold out for the last weekend, but try to take younger children before that. There's also a special children's matinee at 11 a.m. the Saturday before Halloween.

  You'll be welcomed to this nightmare for $5 apiece, adults and teens, $4 for younger kids, $3 each at the Saturday matinee. In 1995, tickets were sold at *Circle K* stores; proceeds benefit the Shakespeare Festival. For more on this talented group, see p. 38. Check the newspaper for other haunted houses and Halloween events.

        🏴 🏴 🏴

A Plethora of Trees

Festival of Trees
Boise Centre on the Grove
Thanksgiving

What started as a minor seasonal offering has become a major event, copied in a dozen Idaho communities. In Boise, the annual **Festival of Trees** is put on by St. Alphonsus hospital over the long Thanksgiving weekend. If you choose your time carefully and take it slowly, you'll have great fun in the service of a good cause.

The festival's raison d'etre is the trees themselves, more than a hundred of them, some decorated by children or other amateurs, many professionally done. Each is unique, a few are strikingly beautiful; collectively they seem touched by magic. People and groups pay to sponsor the trees and have them decorated; they're displayed, judged, and auctioned off. Since the high bidders often donate the trees *again*, many end up warming hospitals, children's homes and senior centers.

But these days, there's more to this festival than trees: elaborate gingerbread houses, decorated wreaths, a wonderful teddy bear collection, shops, food booths and a room for kids' crafts. There's a full schedule of entertainment, including actors portraying animated "dolls." Oh, and Santa, of course!

If it sounds a bit overwhelming, it can be. Finding an uncrowded time is a trick, and traffic patterns around the trees create more chaos than they should. In general, kids love the "dolls," grownups the trees, and all ages the gingerbread houses. The entertainment gets mixed reviews, only the smallest children seem taken with Santa, and it's generally kids from 3 to 7 who like the crafts.

Several smaller communities have followed suit with festivals of their own; check the paper for details. In early to mid-December, don't miss the lighting of the trees at the *Statehouse* and the *Grove*, the latter accompanied by a children's lantern parade and community sing-along.

Here Comes Santa Claus . . .

Holiday Parade
343-6735
November

Bundle up the kids, grab your thermos and head downtown. Boise's **Holiday Parade** kicks off the season with a rousing good parade: more than 150 entries and Santa himself, bringing up the rear.

This Saturday-before-Thanksgiving tradition is fast approaching the half-century mark: 1997 will be its 50th anniversary. It's homegrown and strictly volunteer, with locally-built floats, marching bands, car clubs, horse groups, service clubs and politicians of every stripe. There are no entry fees, and prizes are given for the best floats. The parade starts at 10 a.m. downtown, and usually lasts about two hours.

🏳 🏳 🏳

Deck the Halls!

Holiday Lights Tour
December
345-4354

The newspaper always prints lists of beautifully-lighted homes, and we always go see them. But *someone* has to drive, so *someone* doesn't see much. Now, you can leave the driving to someone else.

The folks at the *Retired Senior Volunteer Program* offer their one-hour **Holiday Lights Tour** four times each evening from early December to New Years. You can choose a west Boise tour aboard a heated trolley, or a frosty-er ride through east Boise on the open air Tour Train, complete with elves, carols, and maybe Santa himself. Tickets are available at *Select-A-Seat* (p. 28): $6 for adults, $4 for children, kids under 2 free. Get your tickets early, because they often sell out.

🏳 🏳 🏳

Just for Fun

Introduction

For many of today's kids, the "hurried child" syndrome is all too literally real: they're whisked from lesson to lesson instead of gathering in the backyard; play T-ball instead of sandlot baseball; take gymnastics and karate instead of playing marbles and kick-the-can; go on field trips to the zoo and the museum instead of exploring on their own.

That's not all bad, certainly. Many of the things that keep their bodies strong and their minds curious didn't exist when we were children, and their lives are the richer for them. But childhood hasn't changed since we were there: kids still need time to just be kids, to have adventures with no loftier goal than having fun. Ironically, it's often those adventures that teach them the most important things of all: how to be a friend, how to control their own bodies, how to conquer their fears and perhaps most important of all, how to laugh with joy.

It goes without saying that all adventures, no matter how "educational," should be fun. Otherwise they're not *adventures*. On these outings, though, fun is the end in itself. In this chapter you'll re-discover things you probably did as a child: you'll paddle a canoe, hit a soft ball and a golf ball, try your wobbly knees on roller skates, stay up late at the drive-in. But you'll also get a few glimpses of the silly fun that's a unique part of today's childhood: you'll discover the joys of "soft playgrounds," laugh and sigh at huge, singing animated animals, try roller blades instead of roller skates, and maybe play laser tag.

If truth be told, this chapter is as much for grownups as for kids. We grownups are often too serious; concerned about living up to our responsibilities, many of us forget how to be silly. But we parents are fortunate to have something our childless colleagues lack: an excuse to be children again. Take advantage of it, because it doesn't last long!

Just for Fun

Play It Again, Sam

Planet Kid
1875 S. Century Way
376-3641

Discovery Zone Funcenter
8567 W. Franklin Rd.
375-3000

Oh, to be three feet tall again! Where were these when *we* were kids? All *I* remember is cold monkey bars and hot slides!

The theory is that parents will pay for a safe, soft, indoor playground, and it seems to work. It works best in winter and on rainy days, of course, but also as an alternative to traditional playgrounds on hot summer afternoons. Yes, it's commercial -- but the kids need the exercise and it beats the heck out of video games, doesn't it?

In a national market dominated by a few big chains, Boise's largest "soft playground" is an anomaly: the humongous, homegrown **Planet Kid** at Wings Center south of Overland off Cole. More elaborate than its competitor, Planet Kid boasts three levels of tubes, tunnels, slides, rings, cargo nets, poles, monkey bars, ball-crawls and bridges. Adults may find it all a bit overwhelming, but kids are in their element.

The main space is for kids from 3 to 12, but there's a smaller play area for the toddler crowd featuring a ball pit and a slide. Socks are required in both areas. While the kids work off energy parents can read, study or work at tables nearby. There's also a simple snack bar offering no cooked foods but more nutritious fare than most.

Planet Kid is open from 10 to 8 Monday through Friday, 10 to 9 on Saturday and noon to 6 on Sunday. Admission is $3.95 per child for unlimited play time. For kids 6 to 10 there's a drop-off plan as well: $7.95 for 2.5 hours of supervised play. Group rates are available, and PK -- it won't surprise you to know -- specializes in birthday parties.

New York-based Viacom, Inc., owns the popular **Discovery Zone** chain; the local DZ is at Fairview and Milwaukee. Restricted to kids 12 and under, Discovery Zone adds a bigger snack bar and kid-size skill games to its "soft playground," and trades on Viacom's association with Hollywood. A recent rage was (what else?) the Mighty Morphin Power Rangers: you could have themed birthday parties, or buy a "wrist activator" that came with an all-summer admission pass to DZ.

The regular charge for kids from 2 to 12 is $4 for unlimited play. Children under a year get in free; 1-year-olds pay $2. Parents must stay in the building, and socks are required. Like Planet Kid, DZ specializes in birthday parties, and both facilities do them well.

Paddle Your Own Canoe

Boat House
Julia Davis Park
343-1141

Looking for something to do with your preschooler on a warm spring afternoon or soft summer evening? Ever seen a 7-year old paddle a canoe? Head for the pond in Julia Davis Park.

On weekends in the spring and fall, and every day in summer, the **Boat House** rents pedalboats and canoes. It's a toss-up: pedalboats require more effort than you might think, but canoes are tippy. Our first try at a canoe, when my daughter was 3, was a disaster; that same year, the pedalboat was an instant hit.

The stand is open from noon to dusk May through September. Boats rent for $5 a half-hour, $7.50 an hour (wear a watch) and come with life jackets for kids which must be worn. The stand sells a few snacks too, but you're probably better off without them in the boat.

The first part of the ride, down a narrow canal, is slow and relaxing: use it to practice steering and look for muskrats. Once on the pond, paddle at will among the ducks and geese, marveling at how close they cut it before they get out of the your way. (My sensitive daughter was sure we were going to hit them; we didn't, and neither will you.) Don't forget to look up; you'll probably see heron, and maybe a hawk.

Batter Up!

Airport Batting Cages
3883 S. Orchard
344-2332 or 344-2008

Got a Little Leaguer in need of batting practice? **Airport Batting Cages** -- also known as Ray Sorenson's Family Fun Center -- has a variety of speeds including slow and fast-pitch baseball and slow and fast-pitch softball. The bats are aluminum, in three sizes; helmets with face guards are supplied and must be worn. You get 20 pitches for $2.

Located on Orchard a half-mile south of I-84 at Exit 52, the place is clean if not terribly attractive. It also features bumper cars, Go-Karts (see below), a 9-hole par 3 golf course and a lighted driving range. The facility is open from 10 a.m. to 10 p.m. every day during the summer, with reduced hours in the spring and fall.

Go, Kart, Go!

Airport Go-Kart Raceway
3883 S. Orchard
344-2332 or 344-2008

Objectively speaking, they're noisy, bumpy and downright boring. But to kids of a certain age . . . well, they're heaven.

The **Airport Go-Kart Raceway** has NASCAR-style cars on a double-lane oval track with a single-lane crossover. Drivers must be 10 years old and 53"; children 3 and up can ride with an adult. The cars are in good shape, with harness-type safety belts. Rides are $5 for 7 minutes or $8 for 15 in a single-seater; add $2 for a double-seater.

The center also features "super collider" bumper cars; they look good, but their track's so small only the very youngest will get a thrill.

Pizza and Prizes

Chuck E. Cheese
6255 Fairview Ave.
322-1833

Po-Jo's
7736 Fairview Ave.
376-6981

Imagine munching on pizza while 47 fun-crazed children run around throwing balls, bouncing in mechanical cars and begging for more tokens, and 6-foot-tall animated bears sing "Love Me Do." If that's your idea of a nightmare, you're not a parent: anyone with kids will recognize the syndrome.

Awful as they sound, these pizza-games-and-prizes outfits do have their place. They're good for working off energy in bad weather, some of the games actually involve a bit of skill, and a few -- like air hockey and skeeball -- are fun for grownups as well. But for a couple of years, my excuse was more selfish: they were those rare places I could talk to other Moms in peace.

From the time our kids were 2 until they started school, my playgroup gathered at Show Biz (now **Chuck E. Cheese's**) every couple of weeks in the winter. Mornings were quiet, lunch was a bargain, and the salad bar helped offset our pizza consumption. Most of all, the kids were safe and happy and we were free to talk.

Chuck E. Cheese's is a national chain. Its stock in trade is decent pizza, rides and games geared to the 9-and-under set, and live shows featuring animated animals. They also have a good salad bar, a couple of sandwich choices and a few video games for older siblings.

The preschool crowd usually sticks with the ball-crawl, the pint-sized rides and the show (which scares a few). But as your offspring approach school age you'll notice a major shift: to the games and the *tickets*, which can be redeemed for junky trinkets. This is bad news, as their token consumption ($.25 apiece) rises dramatically. You can try making it an object lesson, encouraging them to save up their tickets for something that will last more than a day. But if you're like most parents, weaning is the wisest course.

Po-Jo's, at Fairview and Five Mile, is a different animal: big, bright and loud. It's a place you come to play games *with* your kids, not

Just for Fun

to talk to other adults. There are a lot more rides and games than at Chuck E. Cheese's (including bumper cars, a batting cage and "virtual reality") and they're mostly geared to an older set: while preschoolers may feel overwhelmed here, preteens will not have outgrown it.

There's the ubiquitous pizza, as well as sandwiches, nachos and ice cream. And of course there are those tickets: Po-Jo's "redemption center" takes up the entire back wall, and nothing good goes for less than 500. But if you're in the mood for Star Wars and your budget will stand it, this place can perk up a dreary winter afternoon.

🌼 🌼 🌼

Preschool Play

Fort Boise Community Center
700 Robbins Road
384-4486 or 384-4240

Two hours of toddler entertainment for $1? It's true! Every Tuesday and Friday from 9-11, you and your toddler or preschooler can play at **Fort Boise's** drop-in gym for $1 per visit per child. There's no registration required, and no charge for parents. With things to climb on, crawl through and jump from, what more do they need?

The city's *Parks and Recreation Department* also offers art, dance and other classes for toddlers and preschoolers. Call for information, and ask to be put on the mailing list for their *Activity Guide*. For information on activities for teens and older children, see p. 70. For more structured preschool play, the nationally-franchised "parent-child developmental play program" *Gymboree* offers classes at the YWCA for children through age 5. Call them at 343-4647.

🌼 🌼 🌼

Tee Time!

The Fun Spot
Julia Davis Park
343-1141

Fun Center
5290 W. Franklin
345-1898

Golf Mountain
1771 N. Wildwood
327-0780

Putt Hutt
1875 Century Way
376-3641

Boise has four miniature golf courses, each with its own distinct style. There's something so solid and comfortable about playing a round with the kids on a soft summer evening that it's worth trying all of them.

The granddaddy is at the **Fun Spot**. It's good for kids and other neophytes, because the 18 holes are flat and pretty easy (my 7-year-old occasionally makes a hole-in-one), with just enough hazards to add interest. It's open weekends starting around Memorial Day and most days in the summer, and there's a carousel there too. It's future is uncertain, though, so call ahead, and try to avoid the late afternoon heat.

Golf Mountain, on Wildwood north of Fairview and Five Mile, offers two courses (*Fox* and the easier *Skunk*); both are beautifully landscaped. Golf Mountain is (surprise!) hilly and therefore more challenging than the Fun Spot, though its greens are short. Adults will like it better, and most kids over 6 can do well enough to satisfy. There's good shade, but heat and the setting sun can still pose problems. Golf Mountain is open noon to 8:30 Tuesday through Sunday. Play costs $5, with no kid's discount, but you can play *both* courses for that fare. The only bathroom is a Porta-Potty; Golf Mountain is *not* stroller-friendly.

When it's cold or rainy, the **Fun Center**, at Franklin and Orchard, is the place for little ones; it's flat and easy. There's a snack bar, pool tables and air hockey. The four-level indoor **Putt Hutt**, at Wings Center near Cole and Overland, is scheduled to open around Thanksgiving and will be tougher. Hours and prices weren't set when we went to press.

Stayin' Alive

Alive After 5
The Grove
May - September

This after work concert-cum-food fest was easier to take kids to in the early days, before it got so popular. But if you pick the right Wednesday, you can still have a light dinner, dance a bit and be home by 7. Or you can head down to the 8th Street Marketplace for *"Alive 'After' Alive After Five"* and party 'til 10. It's your choice.

Consider two things before electing to go to **Alive After 5**: the temperature, and the kind of music. With the fountain turned off to make room for the crowd, the Grove can be miserably hot; stay away when the mercury hits 90. And even if you tend toward heavy metal, remember that the "harder" the music, the noisier the crowd; try something light.

Get there early if you want chairs, (*very* early for a table with an umbrella), or wait 'til 6:30 when the crowd starts to disperse. You may want to scope out the food in advance: a different restaurant offers reasonably-priced tidbits each week; they're generally delicious, but of varying appeal to kids' palates. Beer, wine, soft drinks and frozen yogurt are also sold. A pleasant alternative is to eat outside at *The Beanery*, if you can find a table; there's no problem finding kid-pleasing food there.

It's getting rare, but once in awhile you'll still see the sight I remember from earlier years: parents and grandparents sitting in the shade, smiling fondly as half-a-dozen toddlers dance themselves silly. (Yes, I was one of them -- the smiling parents, that is.) If you happen to catch a moment like that, you'll judge the evening well spent.

'Round and 'Round They Go . . .

Skateworld
7360 Bethel
Boise
378-8300

Rollerdrome
19 10th Avenue South
Nampa
466-9905

The roller skating rink was one of the shrines of my youth. On Friday nights, the glittering ball revolved, the anthems of the 60's played, and I took my first tentative steps into adolescence.

Today's skating rink is a different place: more in-line than traditional, more androgynous than gender-grouped, more athletic than romantic. But it does retain some of the old atmosphere and in any event -- nostalgia aside -- the changes are welcome.

The Treasure Valley has two rinks: **Rollerdrome**, in Nampa, and **Skateworld**, near Cole and Franklin in Boise. Evenings are still teen heaven, but the elementary set should feel comfortable earlier in the day.

Both rinks rent in-line and traditional skates and sell drinks and snacks. Skateworld charges $4 per person including skates and has a practice strip, a small miniature golf course and video games. In summer it's open from 11 to 7 Monday through Thursday, 1 to midnight Friday and 1 to 7 Saturday. School-year hours are 1 to 9:30 Monday through Thursday, 1 to midnight Friday and Saturday, and 1 to 6 Sunday.

Rollerdrome charges $3 plus $1 for skates. In the summer they're open every afternoon from 1 to 4, Wednesday, Thursday and Sunday night from 7:30 to 10, Friday night from 7:30 to 11 and Saturday night from 7:30 to midnight. The weekday afternoon sessions disappear once school begins, and evenings start at 7 after daylight savings. (If you can keep all *that* straight you're a better man than I am, Gunga Din!)

Two words of wisdom: if you can't get elbow and knee pads on your kids, insist on long pants and sleeves. And don't plan to skate too long the first time: the kids may not tire, but *you* will. (We're *not* getting older; clearly, they've made skating harder than it used to be!)

All Wet!

The Grove
8th & Main

Sometimes a kid just *has* to get wet. And sometimes a parent just *has* to sit and watch, wondering why they aren't 3 anymore.

When you reach that point, the answer is under your nose. The fountain at the **Grove** is the perfect capper to an urban stroll (p. 50), a unique solution to Mom-wants-lunch-but-the-kids-won't-sit-still, or just a goofy little outing in itself. Put bathing suits under clothes, pack dry clothes and a towel, and walk, bus or drive to the corner of 8th and Main.

If you're looking for lunch, go through *The Beanery's* line (great kids' meals, super mashed potatoes, "blushing" applesauce, real milkshakes) and grab an outside table. When you've stuffed as much food as you can down their throats, set them free to play in the fountain and pick up a book, because it's likely you won't see them for awhile.

This is a classic kids' fountain: the kind you can splash in, run through and sit on. Kids invariably make friends there, and most parents are pretty responsible (but beware of marauding bicyclists and skateboarders). When they tire of the fountain, invite them to look inside the log in the stream (it's a badger), or try to guess what the kids in the sculpture are doing (playing marbles; the girl has a bag in her hand.)

You don't *have* to lunch, of course; you can just grab a seat and watch the passing scene. If you forgot to bring reading matter, *Coffee News-Coffee News*, just north up the brick path, has an extensive selection of magazines. And if you simply *must* enlighten the kids, there's history, government and commerce just seconds away.

Goofy as it sounds, this is an adventure every child should have. If they don't get a thrill out of it, they're growing up faster than you think!

The Silver Screen

Parma Motor-Vu	Terrace Drive-in	The Motor-Vu
U.S. 95	3701 Lake Ave.	165 S. 2nd E.
Parma	Caldwell	Mountain Home
722-6401	455-1433	587-5010

Drive-in movies will soon go the way of typewriters, shoelaces and watches with hands -- driven out not so much by technology as economics. Before it's too late, give your kids one of the quintessential experiences of your own youth: staying up *late*, eating bad hot dogs and worse popcorn, and curling up with a blankie in the back seat while Mom and Dad watch the movie. The difference is that now, when it's over, *you* get to gaze at their angelic little faces as you carry them in to bed.

There are three places in the Treasure Valley you can still do that, but all require a bit of a drive: the **Parma Motor-Vu** (a mile north of Parma on 95), the **Terrace Drive-in** in Caldwell and the **Motor-Vu** in Mountain Home. All operate summer only, and you'll need to allow an hour each way. Tickets run $3 or $4, but kids are often admitted free.

The hardest part, of course, is finding a palatable movie. They had *Doris Day* movies at the drive-in when I was a kid, but today, unless you're into gore and super heroes, you'll have to search. With older kids you need a flick they can semi-understand; with little ones, you want one *you'll* understand that won't scare them. (We saw *Big* with our 2-year-old at the now-defunct FairVu; it was perfect on both counts.)

Drive-in aficionados split into two groups: those who bring their own drinks and snacks, and those who firmly believe that eating concession-stand food is an integral part of the experience. (I count myself in the latter group.) Be sure to dress the kids in pajamas and bring blankets, pillows and that special "softie" for the little ones. (Some people bring chairs and sit outside their cars, but *I* think that's cheating.)

Just don't recreate your own youth *too* literally. Drive-in operators tend to frown on adults trying to sneak in in the trunk of someone's car!

Tag!

Q-Zar
2110 Broadway
342-6265

Don't think of it as a war game: they're just high-tech flashlights, and you're just *tagging* your opponents. Yeah, sure. But if you can take it in that spirit, or if you *like* war games, laser tag can be fun.

At **Q-Zar**, you'll sign a release, be fitted with sensor vests, organized into teams and given red or green laser guns. (Very definitely guns, not "flashlights.") In the "environment" your objective is to tag your opponents or their headquarters, temporarily deactivating them. If you're tagged four times you must recharge. The large room is dimly lit and full of day-glo orange tape, with columns, walls and obstacles everywhere. You start at your headquarters at one end of the room and traverse the environment as you dare, trying to shoot and not be shot. Your ultimate goal is to invade and deactivate the other team's headquarters.

A computer prints a personalized score sheet for each player, and therein lies the rub: for a certain group of kids -- mostly teen and preteen males -- laser tag can be addictive. Be prepared to set limits, because it doesn't come cheap. A 15-minute game costs $7 on weekends, $6 on weekdays, though there are coupons, reduced prices in the early evening, "memberships" and "frequent player" discounts.

This certainly isn't for small children, and our 7-year-old was frightened by it. But it does have a certain forbidden appeal that gets your adrenalin going, and I've seen kids about the same age having a great time. Depending on your point of view, it's either offensive or a healthy way for them to work out their aggressions. Caveat emptor.

Q-Zar is open from 10 a.m. to midnight Monday through Thursday, 10 to 1 Friday and Saturday and 11 to 11 on Sunday. It also has a *golf simulator* ($20 an hour for up to five golfers) that puts you on popular PGA courses, a spinning *Orbitron*, a pizza restaurant and a room with pinball and video games. Sadly, most are violent.

Jingle Bells, Jingle Bells . . .

Bogus Creek Outfitters
2405 Bogus Basin Road
922-4158

Idaho City Livery
392-9849

Over the river and through the woods, to Grandmother's house we go. The horse knows the way to carry the sleigh . . .

Or, in this case, *horses* -- two huge Percherons pulling a 28-person sleigh. Grandmother's house never looked like this either: an insulated *Kenyan Cabin* complete with wood stove. But the horses are real, and so are the woods and the snow, and the hot drinks and steak-and-shrimp dinner taste mighty good after that chilly ride.

Bogus Creek Outfitters offers rides-cum-dinner twice a night, at 6 and 8:30, by reservation only. They leave from the First Aid Station at Bogus Basin Ski Resort. The charge is $49 per person.

Dashing through the snow, in a one-horse open sleigh, o'er the fields we go, laughing all the way . . .

To brighten *your* spirits on a cold winter's day, give **Idaho City Livery** a call. They specialize in parties, retreats and dinner rides, but will sometimes take a couple of families for a non-dinner ride if you arrange it in advance. They have a buggy and a wagon as well as a sleigh, so rides are possible all year 'round. For a full day's adventure, try some *ice skating* (p. 74) or *cross-country skiing* (p. 72), then soothe those tired muscles with a soak at *Warm Springs Resort* (p. 128).

Bells on bobtail ring, making spirits bright. What fun it is to ride and sing a sleigh-ing song tonight!

Day Trips

Introduction

Writing about day trips around the Treasure Valley must have something in common with writing songs, at least the way Bob Seger does it: the trick, as he says, is "what to leave in, what to leave out." Even though Idaho has few roads and fewer towns than most states, there's no shortage of places to go, people to see, adventures to have. All you need is your car, a little courage and an abundance of curiosity.

In choosing the adventures for this chapter, safety and amenities played a big role. Adults without children can dare many things that parents, wisely, would hesitate to try. The vast majority of these adventures, therefore, take you on paved roads, with bathrooms, telephones and food stops reasonably available. The few exceptions are places I've ventured to often and am confident of, like *Silver Creek Plunge*, where the road is well-traveled and there's a mobile phone.

A few precautions are nonetheless in order. Never venture any distance without a full tank of gas. Stock your car with emergency provisions: warm clothes, blankets, food and water, a flashlight, maps, matches, pressed logs, a first aid kit. (A cellular phone is great if you have one.) Watch the weather; don't venture out in winter storms and beware of mountain roads during the spring melt. Finally, keep your expectations low: a sick or cranky child may mean a quick retreat to civilization just when you were looking forward to a warm soak.

Most adventures an hour or more away are listed in this section, but a few are elsewhere. A sleigh ride in Idaho City, for example, is combined with a similar ride closer to town and listed in *Just for Fun*. For similar reasons, ice skating and horseback riding in Idaho City are described in *Sports and Recreation*. Happy motoring!

☺ ☺ ☺

Day Trips

More Good Pickins'

Emmett Chamber of Commerce　　**Canyon Co. Extension Agent**
365-3485　　**454-7461**

An apple or cherry-picking trip to Emmett or Canyon County combines pastoral scenery with one of the classic delights of childhood.

We've returned again and again to **Emmett** because we like the drive and the town, but the **Sunny Slope** area of Canyon County offers good u-pick opportunities too. Start by deciding where to go (check this book for nearby adventures), then call one of the places listed below or check the classified ads under "food and produce." If you draw a blank, call one of the numbers listed above or go and look for signs.

Timing is everything, so always call first: Mother Nature doesn't always ripen her produce on schedule. Generally, cherries ripen in June and last several weeks as different varieties reach maturity; apples begin in August and continue through October. Orchards can be hot, so pick a cool day and bring hats and sunglasses. Long pants, sleeves and even gloves help avoid scratches and scrapes. Don't forget to bring your own containers, and use the bathroom before you leave home.

Both fruits require ladder or tree-climbing, so they aren't for small children (though our 2-year-old was delighted to sit on the ground and eat cherries!). Preschoolers usually do fine with the fruit on the lowest branches, while older kids delight in showing off their climbing prowess.

There's picking right near downtown Emmett, but we prefer the views from South Slope (on your left as you come into town). We've had good luck at *Frisbee's, Aganbroad's, Sanders'* and *B & H* (where on weekends you can watch apples pressed into cider and sample the luscious results). In Sunny Slope, try *Robison's* or *Williamson's*.

Allow at least half a day for this adventure. To get to *Emmett*, take Highway 44 (State Street) west; five miles past Eagle, turn right on Idaho 16. For *Sunny Slope*, take I-84 west to Exit 35 (signed for Karcher Mall), follow Highway 55 (Karcher Road) west and turn left on Sunny Slope Road. For u-pick opportunities closer to Boise, see p. 19.

☾ ☾ ☾

Huck Finn Time

Payette River
Horseshoe Bend to Montour

You've floated the Barber-to-Boise (p. 59). You've got your canoe or raft, the kids are water-proofed, and you're ready to get away from the crowds. Say hello to the Payette.

The **Payette River** is navigable most of the way from Banks to its confluence with the Snake at Weiser, and there are several intermediate and advanced floats north of Banks. But it isn't until the river reaches Horseshoe Bend that it becomes truly family-friendly.

This is definitely a two-car adventure; see p. 60 for what to take and how to divide it. Take Highway 44 (State Street) five miles past Eagle; turn right on 16 to Emmett. At the intersection, turn right on 52 and follow it through town; turn right when it does. Just after Black Canyon Dam, Ola Highway goes left; just after that is a road to the right signed for *Montour*. Take it 1.5 miles to the bridge. Leave one car there, retrace your steps and continue northeast to *Horseshoe Bend*: this is the stretch you'll be floating. Watch for the Riverside restaurant as you enter Horseshoe Bend. Leave the second car there and launch.

This isn't a wilderness float; that's not what you're after. This is more like Huck Finn stuff: peaceful, quiet, with civilization nearby in case you get in trouble. The big difference between this and the Boise is that here you may be almost alone. The trip should take about two hours and is pretty consistent all the way: the current gets faster or slower depending on the river's width, but there aren't any waterfalls or major diversions, few overhanging branches and few choices of route.

When your kids are ready for whitewater, the Payette offers several suitable floats -- mostly south of Banks and north of Smiths Ferry. Call a licensed outfitter about your children's ages and abilities.

☉ ☉ ☉

High Road to Heaven

Silver Creek Plunge
Garden Valley
344-8688 or 376-1623

Imagine floating in body-warm water high in the mountains, surrounded by whispering pines. As you stare lazily at the sky, your toddler jumps in and out of waist-high water and your older kids shriek with laughter as their pile of tubes comes tumbling down. You can almost smell the steaks your spouse is grilling on the barbecue.

Silver Creek isn't the Ritz, and it's a two-hour trip over some rough road, but on a cool spring or fall day it has often seemed to me the nearest thing to heaven on this earth. For reasons not entirely clear to me, every kid I've talked to has also named it their favorite pool.

It's a classic mountain "plunge," warmed by geothermal water and surrounded by amenities of varying age and condition. The pool has a natural rock wall, a walled-off toddler section, a cement-bottomed midsection perfect for the 6 to 10 set, and a sandy-bottomed deep end. Like *Givens Hot Springs* (p. 125), Silver Creek's best feature is its temperature: you'll never find the water too cool for comfort; indeed, on hot summer days, it's most pleasant in the morning and evening.

The pool is open from 9 a.m. to 11 p.m. (when the generator goes off as well). It has tubes, a deck with a few tables, plenty of chairs, a small store and a snack bar open weekends only. There are barbecue grills, a swing set, a volleyball net and a small creek on the grounds. In case of emergency, the owner has a mobile phone you can use.

Overnight cabins run $30 to $60 and range from barely-livable A-frames to two-roomers with heat, electricity, kitchens and flush toilets. (You bring linens, dishes and pots and pans.) Tent and RV spaces are also available. The road up is closed to cars from early fall through at least April, but the resort stays open for snowmobilers.

Sadly, Silver Creek's biggest weakness is a parent's nightmare: poor bathroom facilities. There are no showers, and except in the deluxe cabins, only chemical toilets in outdoor Port-A-Potties. There are dressing rooms, but they won't win any prizes for ambiance either.

Besides the usual gear, pack lots of sunblock, all the water toys you can find, and perhaps an umbrella -- on weekends all the available shade gets taken early. If you're staying overnight you may also want the kids' bikes, their fishing poles and maybe your softball gear.

Take food too. The store stocks everything you'd expect of a convenience store catering to campers, but nothing resembling real meals. The snack bar's food is surprisingly good but not very nutritious -- mostly the standard hamburgers, ice cream and soft drinks.

All-day swimming costs $4 for teens and adults and $3 for kids, and *isn't* included in the price of a cabin. There's a $2 swim from 9 to 11 each night, if you're camping in the area or staying in Garden Valley.

Newcomers to mountain roads had best prepare themselves for the last 8 miles. Head out State Street (Highway 44) and take 55 north through Horseshoe Bend to Banks. Turn right on the South Fork Road, and left at the Crouch turnoff. Go through Crouch, gassing up if you need to, and head out the Middle Fork Road (FS 698). In a few miles the pavement turns to gravel. You'll pass Tie Creek, Hardscrabble and Rattlesnake campgrounds. Just past Trail Creek Campground take the fork to the right, signed for Silver Creek. It's eight very long miles uphill on a rutted dirt road. You don't need a 4-wheel drive, but take it easy -- those ruts tend to surprise you. Allow a full two hours for the trip.

☺ ☺ ☺

Great Miners' Ghosts!

Silver City
Owyhee County
(503) 372-3402

Placerville
Boise County
392-6040

Take a day that isn't too hot, kids who aren't too young and parents who aren't too stressed, and a visit to one of Idaho's nearby "ghost" towns can be an excellent adventure.

Silver City is your first choice. The town hosts an open house in September, but you can visit anytime from about May 1 'til the snow flies. Silver City was founded in 1864 when gold was found in nearby Jordan Creek, but a rich vein of silver proved more profitable. Most of its 40 buildings were built in nearby Ruby, but when the mills went in closer to the mines, the buildings were uprooted and Silver City was born. By 1866, the town's mills were processing $70,000 a week.

In its heyday, Silver City had six general stores, eight saloons, a hospital, a brewery, and the Territory's first telegraph and daily newspaper. Mining was a quarrelsome business: in 1868 a dispute between claimholders became an underground war and three people were killed. By the 1930's mining was dying and Silver City was doomed: the county seat was moved to Murphy, electric lines were removed and many of the old buildings were sold for lumber.

The town has never been completely abandoned, though, and since 1990 it's undergone a renaissance. It's an official Historic Preservation District now, with the annual open house as its fundraiser. A donation of $10 per adult and $5 per child is requested.

The finest building in Silver City is the *Idaho Hotel*, built in 1863 and relocated from Ruby the same year. You can still stay overnight (bring linens) or have dinner in the restaurant by reservation. Nearby you'll find the old *Idaho Avalanche* office. Then walk up Morning Star Mill Road to the *Old Schoolhouse Museum*, and behind it to Silver City's first *Catholic Church*. During the open house you'll also get a look at several private homes, partially or completely restored.

Silver City isn't exactly a mecca for kids: the only public bathroom is a bit away from everything and there's a certain lack of tolerance. But older children usually find the town "neat" and the nearby creek fun.

Take I-84 west to Exit 36 and follow signs through Nampa to Highway 45 (12th Avenue South). Turn right on 45 and follow it across the Snake River. Just across the river bear left on 78 to Murphy. The turnoff is on the right, five miles beyond Murphy. Silver City is about 28 miles from there -- most of it dirt and some of it pretty rough. A 4-wheel drive is helpful but not necessary; call 495-2319 for road conditions.

Another possibility is **Placerville**, which boasts a cemetery with elaborate headstones, an intact saloon and other buildings. Take Warm Springs Avenue and Idaho 21 to Idaho City, turn on Main Street and follow the signs on FS 307 through New Centerville to Placerville.

Taking the Plunge

Givens Hot Springs
Marsing
495-2000

If you have yet to experience the pleasures of a "rural plunge," be forewarned: this is *not* the pool at the Beverly Hilton. But **Givens Hot Springs** is clean, friendly and warm -- an oasis in the desert just an hour away. And since when have kids cared about decor?

When I first discovered warm water pools, the idea of a roof overhead seemed an unnecessary intrusion. But I've come to savor the special pleasures of indoor swimming: shelter from the sun, more consistent water temperature, and a steamy "bathhouse" feel that somehow reminds me of my own childhood.

The consistency of the water is Givens' strongest suit. We like it best on nippy fall days, but it's delightful on all but the hottest. The water is always pleasantly warm throughout the pool, and that's rarer than you might think: many's the time we've trekked to a plunge only to find the water too warm or too cool, or full of hot and cold spots.

For families with young children Givens' best feature is its large toddler pool, separated from the main pool by a low wall. The main pool in turn is divided by a rope into shallow and deep sections; children must be accompanied by an adult or able to prove they can swim to be allowed in the deep end. There's no diving board, but diving is allowed in the deep end, and there are rubber balls for play. (When it's crowded, getting hit on the head is a real possibility.) You can also bring your own toys, but according to a state law flotation devices are permitted only in the toddler pool unless they have a seat (rafts qualify).

The combination bath and changing rooms are adequate -- and considerably better than *Silver Creek's* (p. 121). There are private booths with benches for changing, a sink, and showers that usually work well enough for a quick rinse and shampoo. Belongings can be left at the poolside snack bar in bags provided by the management. The snack bar offers mostly standard fare: candy, ice cream, chips and soft drinks. In a pinch, the microwaved pizza and pita sandwiches aren't bad.

A swim costs $4 for adults and $2 for children; season passes are available. You can rent a private room with large tub, but the fare is pretty steep: $4 an hour *per person*. I can't recommend the tiny cabins, but camping (RV or tent) is fine. There are swings, horseshoe pits, a volleyball net, a baseball diamond, barbecue grills, tables and plenty of trees for shade. Charcoal and lighter fluid are sold at the snack bar.

The place has a rich history. The Givens family settled here around 1880 and ten years later built a bathhouse. Fortuitously located between Boise and the mining boom town of Silver City, it flourished: at its height it boasted a hotel, restaurant, ice cream parlor, barbershop and post office! The hotel burned in 1939 and the graceful bathhouse was torn down in the 50's and replaced by the current cinderblock structure. The springs are still operated by descendants of the original owners.

You can easily drive from Boise, have a relaxed swim and return in half a day. For a full day's outing, consider combining a swim with a look at *Kuna Cave* (p. 17) or a search for wild asparagus (p. 12). Don't try to go to *Silver City*, though; that's a full day's trip in itself (p. 123).

From Boise head west on I-84 to Exit 36. Follow the signs through Nampa to Highway 45 (12th Avenue South). Turn right (south) on 45 and follow it across the Snake River. Just past the river, turn right at the sign on Highway 78. Givens is eight miles from there.

Now THIS is a Sandbox!

Bruneau Dunes State Park
Bruneau
366-7919

You've broken out the fishing poles, the camping gear is all loaded, the kids have spring fever -- and it's 60 degrees out. Don't despair; head for **Bruneau Dunes State Park**.

Home to the highest sand dunes in North America, Bruneau's 600 acres are perfect for hiking, camping, fishing and just generally working off the winter blahs. The kids will entertain themselves for hours climbing the dunes and sliding down again, but you can also take a short nature walk, hike a five-mile trail around the dunes, boat on Dune Lake and fish for largemouth bass and bluegill. You're sure to see water fowl, and you might spot coyotes, jackrabbits or kangaroo rats.

The dunes come from sand and lava rock that began to collect in the circular basin after the Bonneville Flood some 30,000 years ago. They stand almost 500' tall and are constantly changing shape.

The Visitor's Center, open from 8:30 to 5 daily March through October, has exhibits of local plants, wildlife and geology. Admission to the park is $2 a carload; campsites go for $9 without hookups, $12 with.

Watch out for three things here: heat, bugs and wind. (It was so windy once that we couldn't get our tent up and went to a motel instead!) And plan to take showers and vacuum the car when you get home.

Bruneau is 20 miles southeast of Mountain Home. Take I-84 east to Exit 90 and follow Business 84 through Mountain Home. Turn right on 51/67 (Grandview Road) and follow 51 left across the Snake River. Just after you cross, turn left on 78; it's two miles to the park.

☉ ☉ ☉

Splash!

Warm Springs Resort
Idaho City
392-4437

Picture yourself swimming lazily in warm water, snow all around, the air so steamy it's like a cozy cocoon: that's **Warm Springs Resort** at its best. It is, at least, if you're a parent; kids, who lack appreciation for the subtler things in life, like it best in the bright summer sun!

Nestled in the mountains just an hour from Boise, the area's best-known and most popular geothermal swimming pool should be an ideal getaway, and most of the time it is. But once in awhile, just when you most need a warm soak, you'll find the water too cool for comfort.

Still, the large outdoor pool is pleasant and there's a separate wading pool for toddlers. The dressing rooms, showers and toilets are adequate, and there's a pretty good snack bar (no food or drink at the pool, though). All summer, there's an unexpected bonus: hummingbirds feed right outside the snack bar windows! We could wish, though, for a few more poolside chairs, and maybe an umbrella or two.

Warm Springs is open from 10 a.m. to 10 p.m. Wednesday through Monday, closed on Tuesdays. Take Warm Springs Avenue and Idaho 21 past Grayback Gulch campground; soon after the road widens and straightens out, you'll see the sign for Warm Springs Resort on your left. (If you get to Idaho City, you've gone about a mile too far.) Warm Springs has tent and RV camping and a few cabins. There's *horseback riding* nearby (p. 68), and a warm soak is especially pleasant after an afternoon of *ice skating* (p. 74) or *skiing* (p. 72).

☺ ☺ ☺

Soak Your Body

Pine Flats Hot Springs
West of Lowman

Kirkham Hot Springs
Northeast of Lowman

Hot-springing has been an avocation with me ever since I came to Idaho, and the source of many adventures for our family. One early outing reminded me that I "wasn't in Kansas anymore."

It was March; I'd been in Idaho two months when friends took me to *Bonneville Hot Springs*, 20 miles north of Lowman. We had a pleasant drive up and a lovely soak, but at 5 p.m. it was getting dark and the car was stuck in the snow. It was then I realized that we hadn't passed a car for the last 20 miles!

We got out, but that was the one and only time I ventured into Idaho's outback unprepared, and I don't recommend it. Summer and winter, my car now carries boots, socks, gloves, sweaters, flashlights, matches, blankets, food and water, a first aid kit and a set of maps. I've never needed any of them, but I feel better knowing they're there!

Soaking in 100-degree water in the middle of nowhere is my idea of heaven, but it's not without its caveats. Most pools have enough flow-through to stay fairly sanitary, but you do see things floating by and sensitive skin may itch. (Rinsing helps.) Certain springs become party places after dark, so daylight hours are generally best for kids. And whether or not you skinny-dip, you may encounter others who do.

You're unlikely to run into trouble at **Pine Flats**: large, popular and close to civilization, it makes an excellent first "dip." You can either take Idaho 21 to Lowman and go four miles west on the South Fork Road, or take 55 to Banks and go east 19 miles. The springs are an easy .3 mile walk on a well-worn path from the west end of the campground. Geothermal water cascades down a 100' cliff, forming pools of various temperatures. The best ones (complete with shower) are around the point of the cliff: if the river is high, you'll have to climb.

These springs are so popular you'll rarely have them to yourself, which may be a plus if your kids meet other kids. It's also popular enough that bathing suits have become the norm, and you don't have to worry about being warm enough: on a hot day, it's often *too* warm.

Kirkham is another popular, easy-to-get-to spring. Take 21 four miles northeast from Lowman and watch for the sign on your right. You'll cross a small bridge to a rather unattractive campground; the springs are down a trail at the southwest end. Depending on the crowd, you'll have your choice of several pools ranging from warm to hot, with or without showers. On hot days swimmers often cool themselves in the river, but beware of letting children do this without close supervision.

Unlike adults, who tend to laze, kids use hot springs like tiny swimming pools: they jump in and out, fill and dump buckets and splash endlessly. It's up to you whether they put their faces in, but don't let them drink -- which they probably won't want to do anyway.

Besides the obvious bathing suits, towels and sunblock, the most important thing is shoes: nylon or canvas deck shoes with good traction, since you'll probably be climbing on slippery algae. Insist that everyone wear shoes in the pool as well: you never know what might be on the bottom. For sensitive skin, bring clean rinse water and a soothing lotion. And keep in mind that hot water relaxes the muscles, so get up slowly.

If you enjoy hot-springing there are others you'll want to try; consider buying a book that lists them. There's a small spring at *Hot Springs Campground* four miles east of Crouch on the South Fork Road, another small one 8.5 miles west of that, and several along the *Middle Fork Road* north of Crouch. Another hot springs highway is *FS 268*, along the Middle Fork of the Boise: there are at least five on the way to Atlanta and two beyond, but be warned -- this is 50 miles of bad road.

☉ ☉ ☉

Index

Alive After 5	111
Ann Morrison Park	8, 59, 62, 80, 90
Art in the Park	98
Arts for Kids	85
Asparagus	12
Assay Office	49
Autumn	22, 119
BSU	36, 40, 56, 69
Ballet Idaho	39
Banks	121, 129
Barber Park	20, 59, 62, 67
Baseball	71, 107
Basque Museum	50, 52
Biking	62, 64
Birds of Prey	9, 66
Boats	106
Bogus Basin Ski Resort	72
Bogus Creek Outfitters	68, 116
Boise Art Museum	30
Boise Basin Trail Rides	68
Boise Family YMCA	70
Boise Hawks	71
Boise Music Week	81
Boise National Forest	25
Boise Opera	29
Boise Philharmonic	31, 79
Boise River	7, 20, 57, 58, 59, 61
Boise River Festival	90
Boise River Greenbelt	62, 67
Boise SummerFest	36
Boise Tour Train	43
Bonneville Point	44
Book Stores	3
Botanical Garden	16
Bown House	83
Bruneau Dunes State Park	127
Butterflies	14
Caldwell	58, 66, 94, 97, 114, 119
Caldwell Night Rodeo	94
Cascade	25, 97
Caterpillars	14
Caving	17
Ceramica	37
Cheese	23

Christmas	25, 40, 101, 102
Christmas trees	25
Chuck E. Cheese	108
Coasting	75
Cross-country skiing	72
Crouch	121, 129
Dairy Days	87
Deer Flat National Wildlife Refuge	65
Deli Days	89
Discovery Center of Idaho	6
Discovery Zone Funcenter	105
Drive-in movies	114
Ducks	8
Eagle	18, 35, 57, 61, 87
Eagle Fun Days	87
Eagle Island State Park	57
Easter	80
Egyptian Theater	50, 81, 82
8th Street Public Market	18
Emmett	18, 25, 88, 97, 119, 120
Emmett Cherry Festival	88
Festival of Trees	101
Fiddlers	92
Fireworks	90, 93
First Night	78
First Thursday	32
Fort Boise Community Center	70, 109
Fourth of July	93
Frogs	13
Fruit	18, 19, 119
Fun Center	110
Fun Spot	8, 106, 110
Garden City	34
Gardens	7, 16
Geology	11
Ghost towns	123
Givens Hot Springs	125
Glenns Ferry	95, 97
Go-Karts	107
Golf Mountain	110
Greek Food Festival	84
Greenbelt	20, 58, 62, 67
Grove	50, 111, 113
Gymboree	109

Index

Halloween	19, 100
Hiking	20, 22, 65
Historic Preservation Week	82, 83
Holiday Lights Tour	102
Holiday Parade	102
Horseback Riding	68
Horseshoe Bend	120
Hot springs	121, 125, 128, 129
Hulls Gulch	64, 65
Hyde Park Street Fair	99
IJA Productions	33, 78
Ice skating	74
Idaho Botanical Garden	16
Idaho City	25, 68, 72, 74, 86, 116, 128
Idaho City Arts & Crafts Festival	86
Idaho City Livery	116
Idaho Public TeleVision	24
Idaho Shakespeare Festival	38, 100
Idaho State Historical Museum	45
Idaho Statehouse	47
Idaho Theater for Youth	40
Jaialdi	52
Julia Davis Park	8, 10, 43, 45, 81, 90, 98, 106, 110
Kathryn Albertson Park	22
Kirkham Hot Springs	129
Kuna	12, 17, 18, 35, 66
Kuna Cave	17
Lake Lowell	58, 66
Laser tag	115
Libraries	34, 35
Lowman	25, 129
Lucky Peak	57, 58
MK Nature Center	7
Markets	18
Marsing	125
Meridian	23, 34, 87
Meridian Dairy Days	87
Middleton	61
Miniature Golf	110
Mining	11, 86, 123
Mores Mountain	22, 64, 65
Mountain biking	64
Mountain Home	25, 44, 114, 127
Museum of Mining & Geology	11

Music Week	81
Nampa	18, 23, 58, 66, 94
Natatorium	55
National Oldtime Fiddlers' Contest	92
Nature Center	7
New Plymouth	97
Nightmare on 9th Street	100
Oinkari Basque Dancers	52
Old Assay Office	49
Old Boise	50
Old Idaho Penitentiary	46
Oregon Trail	44, 95
Parades	87, 88, 90, 92, 93, 102
Parma	114
Payette River	120, 121, 129
Pine Flats Hot Springs	129
Pinnacle	69
Placerville	124
Planet Kid	105
Po-Jo's	108
Puppets	29, 40
Putt Hutt	110
Q-Zar	115
REI	69
Rafting	59, 61, 120
Rockclimbing	69
Rodeo	94
Roller blading	67, 112
Rollerdrome	112
Roller skating	67, 112
Sandy Point	58
Shakespeare	38
Silver City	123
Silver Creek Plunge	121
Skateworld	112
Skiing	72
Sledding	75
Sleigh rides	116
Snake River Stampede	94
Snowboarding	72
Star	34, 61
Stars	21
Storytelling	34

Index

SummerFest	36
Swimming	55, 57, 58, 121, 125, 128
Swiss Village Cheese	23
Tadpoles	13
Three Island Crossing	95
Trail Rides	68
Tour Train	43
Trains	43, 21
Tubing	59, 61, 120
Union Pacific Train Depot	51
Warm Springs Resort	128
Water slides	55, 57
Weiser	92, 97
Western Idaho Fair	96
Wheels R Fun	59, 62, 67
World Center for Birds of Prey	9
YMCA	56, 70
Zoo Boise	10